THE HOME INSPECTION WORKBOOK

The indispensable guide to home inspection that can save you thousands of dollars when you are in the market for a new home, a second home, or merely a sound investment.

by
STEVE HUNTER

HAMMOND INCORPORATED   MAPLEWOOD, NEW JERSEY

THE HOME INSPECTION WORKBOOK

Library of Congress Cataloging in Publication Data

Hunter, Steve.
The home inspection workbook.

"The indispensable guide to home inspection
that can save you thousands of dollars when you
are in the market for a new home, a second home,
or merely a sound investment."

Bibliography: p.
Includes index.
1. Dwellings—Inspection.   I. Title.
TH4817.5.H86   643'.1   79-28692
ISBN 0-8437-3345-4

Printed in the United States of America

CONTENTS

FOREWORD

As thousands of homeowners have discovered, there's many a slip 'twixt the sale and the satisfaction.

Since it is human beings who make the sales, turn out the materials and construct the houses, this condition will persist. To expect otherwise would require earthly perfection, the existence of which would have put the eraser industry out of business a long time ago.

New house warranties and consumer action groups have reduced the chances of winding up with a troublesome house without recourse, but the road to acceptable reparation can be rocky indeed. How much wiser to avoid the pitfalls that sometimes confront the buyer!

You can hire a house analyst, such as the author of this book. Or you can read the book and become your own building inspector. Or you can use an analyst but learn enough to doublecheck his report, giving you a measure of personal satisfaction as well as providing still another means of sidestepping possible trouble. The knowledge gained from reading Steve Hunter's detailed guide on house inspection also will prove invaluable when time forces repairs long after there is any possibility of appeal or reclamation of any sort.

Hunter takes the time and the space to break down the components of a house into small parts. As you read, you will discover that you are absorbing all kinds of information — not only on how to inspect a house, but on how things are made and what makes them tick. The writing is clear, so there is no mistaking Hunter's meaning.

A major plus in learning how to inspect a house is that, once you have learned how to do it, your knowledge will stand you in good stead no matter which type of house you are examining. Contrast this with the situation in the auto repair business, where an expert on one kind of car may have to attend a training school to learn the complexities of another make. The fundamentals of construction are similar in ranches, two-story houses, split levels, high ranches, or the many amalgamated styles on the market. Whatever minor differences exist are discussed plainly in this book.

Since the people who act as sales brokers do not have to be enlightened about the details of house construction, it is well that you should be.

— Andy Lang

HOW TO USE THIS BOOK

Before you select a particular house, you should read carefully the Introduction and Chapters One and Two.

Then sign a contract to buy a house, "subject to satisfactory inspection." (See Chapter Two.) Next, read Chapters Three through Nine and use them to guide you through a step-by-step inspection. Finally, use Chapter Ten to help you evaluate what you have found out about the house from your inspection.

Note: For the convenience of the reader, a set of detachable check sheets is provided at the back of the book.

ACKNOWLEDGMENTS

Among the many I would like to recognize for their help in the inception and completion of this book, the first is Jamie Tombaugh. Years ago, when I needed a bigger house, he said the magic words: "Build it yourself." Jim Tait, who introduced me to real estate investment, has been a guide for years and was kind enough to give me continuing advice on the book as it evolved. Ray Willms, partner, co-worker, and friend, has taught me much about remodeling and repair.

For their generous advice on various subjects I would also like to thank David Kelty of Domus Consultants, Inc., Steve Gross of Consumer Inspection Service, Harry Novinger of Evaluated Home Inspections—all of Denver, Colorado. Jan Kreider, of Boulder, Colorado, shared a particle of his vast solar heating wisdom with me, while Robert Rhoads, of Roswell, New Mexico, educated me on the perils of hard water.

Finally, special thanks go to Mila Mitchell and to Curtis Casewit, without whose advice and encouragement, separately indispensable, there would have been no *Home Inspection Workbook*.

INTRODUCTION

Home buyers are subject to romantic impulses. No one knows this better than I do. I bought my first house fifteen years ago because of its charming location on a wooded hillside. Before long, I found out that the heating was inadequate, and water ran through the basement when it rained. My septic field, the lowest spot in the neighborhood, turned into a foul-smelling lake for six months until spring. In spite of these defects, I was foolish enough to love the house and (as you might expect) sold it for a tidy profit several years later.

When I used the proceeds of the sale of this house to finance my first apartment building, I hired a professional building consultant. His one-hour visit cost me $100 and saved me $300 the same day. He climbed on the roof and found a defect in the roof coating. Sure enough, the roof was under warranty; the roofing contractor who had done the job repaired the original oversight and didn't charge me a dime.

A good inspector's report may be worth many times the cost of his services. If inspection reveals significant defects in a house, you, the buyer, can bargain with the seller for a considerable reduction in the price. Or you may be able to persuade him to undertake the necessary repairs before you buy. A careful inspection can uncover a multitude of problems: broken window hardware, doors that stick, rusty plumbing, a damp basement. You should know about these before you decide to buy; you should know how much it will cost to fix them, or whether you ought to look for a house in better condition.

If you decide to hire a home inspection consultant, try to get a personal recommendation first. Your realtor may know a good inspector. However you locate him, ask about his qualifications and what he will inspect. He may be an engineer, an architect, a plumber, an electrician, or a contractor. He may, like myself, have experience in many fields. Ask whether you will be welcome to follow around on his inspection tour, and have him educate you about your prospective house.

Personally, I believe that no one is better motivated to do a careful job of inspecting a house than the prospective owner: yourself. No one better deserves to be well informed about a house than the person who is going to live in it. Even if you aren't a "handyman" (or "handywoman"), you can use your eyes, ears, and nose carefully. This book will guide you to inspect your own house properly. It's designed to show you what to look for and how to look for it, to teach you some simple tricks of the inspection trade, to help you distinguish major defects from minor inconveniences. At the end of the process you will know more about the house than the real estate agent, and probably more than the seller. You will have the satisfaction and the confidence that comes with taking responsibility for one of life's major financial decisions — buying your own home.

LOCATION
Your first consideration in looking for a home will be its location. You want to choose an environment which is compatible with your interests, and is located as close to shopping, schools, entertainment, and your place of employment as you wish to be. As you narrow your search to a particular house, try to get the best feeling you can about its neighborhood. Ideally, you should talk to some of the neighbors. Ask them pointedly whether there's anything you should know about before buying a house there: Are the other neighbors compatible? Is the area subject to flooding, unstable soils, or nuisances like airport noise?

Drive and walk around the area. If you are next to a school or a shopping center, the traffic may bother you. The dust from playgrounds and parking lots will keep your house dirty. If you are near a hospital or the main avenue to one, expect to hear sirens at all hours.

Industries and airports are greater threats, not only to peace and quiet, but to property values as well. The smokestacks of a large factory can be hidden by foliage in summer, only to appear in autumn when the trees drop their leaves, much to your dismay. Unlikely? Well, it happened to me. Your house may be under the landing approach to an airport several miles away. The planes might come overhead only when certain weather conditions prevail, but during those times you could have them overhead constantly for hours. If you are going to locate within five miles of a major airport, examine a map that shows your location in relation to the runways. Call the airport traffic control to find out which are the ones generally used. If you're not under takeoff and landing patterns, you can live close to it and hardly notice the noise.

Is your prospective home located in the flood plain of a river or creek? Just because other houses have been built there doesn't mean that a "fifty-year flood" can't occur next year. Sad to say, there are builders unscrupulous enough to construct houses, apartments, and even nursing homes in areas that flooded only a few years earlier.

Other hazards to consider include sports stadiums, churches (their traffic can be overwhelming before and after services), sewage treatment plants, scrap yards, refineries, land-fills, power stations, pulp mills, steel smelters, open-pit mines, quarries, elevated freeways, and railroad yards. Some of us may have to put up with one or another of these in our neighborhoods, but knowing about them beforehand is better than finding out later why the house was such a "bargain."

NEW HOME OR OLDER HOME?

In some respects you are better protected when buying a new home. In most states you will be protected by legal requirements that the builder should not have been negligent in construction and finishing, that he should not have fraudulently concealed any defect, and by the theory of "implied warranty" against faults that develop after you buy a new house. This legal protection only pertains if you buy directly from the builder or developer, not a subsequent owner. Any such legal bases for recovery of damages exist only as long as you did not know of any actual or potentially deleterious condition before you bought the house. If you should have to sue the builder, be warned that he may file a countersuit against you to allege that something you may have done damaged the house.

If you buy a new house, you must inspect it just as carefully as you would an older house. Some building inspectors even charge more to inspect a new house than an older one. One of the greatest potential dangers with a new house is that it may be built on unstable soil. New houses are frequently sited on marginal locations, such as on compacted fill dirt and near potential landslides. A rare but not unknown problem is sinking of the earth in areas that have been the scene of extensive mining or removal of underground water or petroleum reserves. In old coal-mining areas, entire towns have sunk into the earth when abandoned galleries collapsed. Shorefront neighborhoods in Southern California are sinking into the sea as a result of oil extraction from onshore and offshore pumping.

One of the most insidious problems is that of shrinking and expanding soil. This causes more damage to homes and other structures than earthquakes, tornadoes, hurricanes, and floods combined — more than twice the amount of damage in monetary terms. Ten percent of all new homes, geologists predict, will suffer severe damage from unstable soil. The worst culprits are clays whose fine particles can absorb vast quantities of water and expand up to fifteen times their dry volume. One variety is known by the scientific term "montmorillonite" or "bentonite." Other kinds of swelling and shrinking soils include gypsum and "white alkali."

Contact the local office of the U. S. Department of Housing and Urban Development, the Veterans Administration, the U. S. Geological Survey, and state agencies such as a state geological survey or division of housing, or local governmental planning and building departments if you have any reason to suspect geological problems in your area.

You can ask for the soil condition report of a registered professional soils engineer when you buy a new house. Such reports are usually required by federal, state, or local agencies. If the builder can't furnish it, the county or city planning office may have a copy. When soil conditions are reportedly unstable, ask the builder for assurance that the foundation was appropriately designed for the conditions.

If you're buying an older home, one more than ten years old will probably have begun to manifest signs of structural distress if it's built on unstable soil without proper design. We'll discuss how to recognize these signs in Chapter Three. It's the one- to nine-year-old house that should be researched carefully to be sure it has been designed to withstand unstable soil conditions, if they exist in your locality. Ask the neighbors whether they have experienced settling, or heaving foundation walls or basement floors. Telephone your local government planning office to find out where problem areas are.

While in some areas of the country at certain periods, shoddy housing was constructed, the majority of the houses constructed between, say, 1890 and 1950 in this country were very well built. A house of this vintage, if well cared for, may be superior to one built since 1960. Nevertheless, be prepared for some inconveniences in an older home. If it was constructed before about 1935, unless the wiring has been updated, you may not find 240-volt current (for clothes dryer, air conditioner, range, and heavy power tools). You may have few electrical outlets in the living room, perhaps only one outlet per bedroom, and none in the bathroom. The plumbing in an older house may require attention, as older pipes and fittings of galvanized steel begin to corrode. But the advantages of solid construction; a more individual floor plan; generous ceiling heights (instead of the unvarying contemporary eight-foot consensus); and such amenities as built-in cupboards, bookshelves, and fireplaces; and attics and basements can more than compensate you for the expense you may have to incur to bring wiring and plumbing up to date.

Consider the amount of fixing up you are prepared to undertake on your house. If you will be satisfied with nothing less than a house in perfect condition, this book will help you find it. If it's less than perfect, you'll have to decide whether your skills and pocketbook match the work to be accomplished. Will you repaint, replace carpets, put up new wallpaper? Can you fix leaky faucets, dripping or stopped-up drains, stuck windows? Many houses are in need of minor repairs here and there, but when a house has many obvious little defects, look even more carefully at the major systems like the furnace and plumbing. If the owner has neglected the little things, it's reasonable to assume that the big things need attention too.

If you're willing to look long enough, you can find an older home that has been cared for splendidly. Perhaps the owner was a plumber, electrician, or contractor who brought everything up to the most recent requirements of the building code!

As you go looking for a house, keep the following general considerations in mind:

X

SITE ORIENTATION

Two identical houses on adjacent lots may have substantially different heating and cooling requirements if they face in different directions. Consider the orientation of your house on its site. A home with its long axis running east-west will gain more heat from the sun in the winter, yet will escape excessive heating on summer afternoons when the sun is in the northwest. Deciduous shade trees on the south and west will cool in the summer but let sunshine through in the winter. On the other hand, their leaves will litter your yard in the autumn, and clog your gutters too.

You should also take into account the orientation of the house with respect to expected summer and winter storms, and the direction of the prevailing winds; and what protection may be afforded by trees and neighboring buildings.

HOUSE DESIGN

Before you sign the contract, be sure you've found the right house for your particular needs. Is the kitchen convenient to an entrance, near the garage or driveway to make it easy to bring in groceries and take out the trash? Does the floor plan allow for access to bedrooms without people tracking through the living room or an intermediate room? Does a hall or closet insulate children's bedrooms from living room noise, so that they can sleep while you're entertaining?

An entrance foyer is convenient, with perhaps a clothes closet near the front door for coats, umbrellas, and the like. A basement, utility room, garage, or attic will be necessary as storage space for out-of-season clothes, sports equipment, yard and garden tools, storm windows, luggage, and whatever. If you're going to use an attic, be sure it has easy access by a stairway, and a usable door.

Does your house have enough bathrooms? Years ago, one bathroom was considered adequate for a house of almost any size, and it was often on the second floor. Today you should have at least a half-bath (with toilet and sink) near the living room, and a minimum of one full bath for every two bedrooms. It's a plus if the master bedroom has a private bath.

Is the house big enough for everyone in your family to have sufficient privacy? Will teenage children have their own bedrooms? Will adult relatives who may live with you require their own private entrance?

Does some member of the family have a noisy or messy hobby or profession, with special requirements as to space and facilities (for example, musical practice, pottery, sculpture, carpentry)?

Another concern will be whether all sleeping rooms have unencumbered exits in case of fire: windows on the ground floor which open, stairways direct and accessible.

Security is an increasing problem these days. Make sure that doors and windows are substantially made and strong enough to lock securely, and that locks and latches are in workable condition. You may wish to consider whether windows are located where they can easily be reached from the outside. Basement windows are especially vulnerable and may require protection in the form of heavy screens or bars.

If your house doesn't have all of the features you want, you may contemplate remodeling. Three of the most common remodeling projects involve enlarging the kitchen, adding an extra bathroom, and finishing a basement or attic into an extra bedroom or den. Remember, it is usually cheaper to remodel existing space inside the house than to construct additions which will require new foundations, walls, and roof.

Watch for unused or low-value areas such as closets, porches, or under-stairs space which can serve for a kitchen expansion or a half-bath. If you plan to remodel a basement, be sure it does not have too low a ceiling, overhead pipes, and heat distribution equipment that will limit or inconvenience your plans. Don't blithely plan to relocate an old furnace to give yourself more space in a basement unless you are willing to contemplate purchasing a new furnace, and replacing hot-air runs, pipes, etc., for example, which may be necessary. Similarly, watch out for attics with cramped head room, poor ventilation, and inadequate floor joists.

CHAPTER ONE: UNDERSTANDING YOUR HOUSE

A house is a collection of systems to shelter us and provide us with services. Many of these haven't changed all that much since the days of the Romans. They had indoor kitchens and baths, lead water pipes, brick walls, tile roofs, gutters, and even central heating! The timber house developed later on, in Europe during the Middle Ages. The nineteenth century gave us galvanized plumbing, flush toilets, gas and oil furnaces. This century added air conditioning and automatic controls that made thermostats, water heaters, and electrical wiring commonplace. Even the most elaborate home today, however, is much less complicated and easier to understand than an automobile.

In this chapter we will survey the general functions of heating, insulation, cooling, and ventilation that characterize a good house, and consider the protection of the house from damage by the elements, water in particular.

1

HEATING YOUR HOUSE

Depending on availability, any of the following fuels or energy sources may be used in your house. Each has characteristic advantages and disadvantages.

GAS

A clean fuel with low maintenance costs. Natural gas has been inexpensive in the past, but it is rising steeply in cost. Liquified or bottled gas is more expensive.

ELECTRICITY

Clean, low maintenance, and cheaper to install than other fuel systems (electricity is not really a "fuel"). Electric heat operates on the resistance principle, using heating coils in a stream of air or by heating a fluid (*hydronically*) which transfers heat to rooms by means of baseboard units or radiators. Electric heat requires no flue, as there are no exhaust gases. Except in the Pacific Northwest, it is expensive.

OIL

For years, oil has been a favorite in the East and the North. It is increasingly subject to fluctuations in supply and price, as we depend more on foreign sources. An oil furnace may use either number two grade oil or number one (the fuel required should be stamped on the furnace plate). Number one is lighter, contains slightly less heat value, and is more expensive. It's generally used in pot-type burners, which may not require electric power to vaporize the oil. Number two is the more popular fuel. It is vaporized or atomized by a pump or blower before ignition in the furnace. Either kind of oil is easy to store and use, and leaves no ash. Oil furnaces should be adjusted by a serviceman for maximum efficiency.

COAL

In areas near coal fields, coal is the cheapest fuel. It is dirty to handle, and requires more handling to feed the stoker and clean out the furnace. Some areas may restrict its use under clean air laws, and smokeless solid fuel such as coke may be allowed.

WOOD

Unless you have a free supply and plenty of time to cut, stack, and feed wood into your furnace or stoves, forget it. It is a labor-intensive fuel and its cost is rising sharply in many areas.

SOLAR

A new house with integral solar energy heating could be an excellent investment, but beware of solar systems grafted onto older homes, especially if the work has been done by amateurs. A solar system should pay back its higher initial cost in five to fifteen years, depending on the location and the price of energy. It may be cost-effective even in areas of low sunshine, such as Boston and New England, because the price of fuel is so high there. Where fuel costs less and sunshine is infrequent, such as in the Pacific Northwest or the Great Lakes region, solar energy may not be economical. All solar systems require a conventional furnace for "back-up" use in emergencies or cloudy weather.

DISTRIBUTION SYSTEMS
Most of the above fuels or sources of heat can be linked with any of the following distribution systems, each of which has its characteristic advantages.

WARM AIR, GRAVITY

The simplest of distribution systems. It is easy to maintain and has few controls except a thermostat and a high-temperature limit switch in the top (plenum) of the furnace. Frequently found in older homes, a gravity system has no filter, so the circulating air will carry dust. This system typically heats the house unequally, so you will find cold areas near windows, and in rooms farthest from the center of the house. Heat will fluctuate somewhat. It cannot be combined with a central air conditioner.

3

WARM AIR, FORCED

The modern descendant of the above, and perhaps the most widely used system in the United States. All forced-air systems are similar. They are automatically controlled by thermostat, fan, and limit switches. When the thermostat signals a drop below selected room temperature, the main burner in the combustion chamber switches on, heating up the air around the heat exchanger in the furnace. When the air is warm enough, the fan-control switch activates the furnace blower, which draws cool air from the rooms through return air ducts. The cool air passes through a filter and over the heat exchanger where it is warmed, past a humidifier where it picks up moisture, and then is forced into the rooms through the warm air runs (or ducts) and registers. As the heated air warms rooms to the desired temperature, the thermostat shuts off the burner, but the blower will continue to run, almost continuously in cold weather, to keep the air from stratifying with the warm air left near the ceiling. A limit control in the furnace shuts off the burner to prevent furnace overheating. Some units will lack filters or humidifiers. The drawbacks to forced air are a degree of heat fluctuation, and the sensation of blowing air, sometimes with noise from the blower as it turns on and off. It can easily be combined with a central air conditioner.

HOT WATER, GRAVITY

This system uses radiators, which some people consider unsightly. It's characteristically a low-maintenance, higher-cost installation until a pipe or valve rusts out (but I know of many 75-year-old systems operating reliably). It is considered very comfortable, with no heat fluctuations, and is quiet. It takes a long time to respond to outside temperature changes.

HOT WATER, PUMPED

Similar to gravity hot water, but the heat is more even and can reach lateral distances from the central furnace. Frequently used in large multi-unit buildings that have a central heating system. It has a pump, which will require maintenance. It may use radiators or baseboard units.

STEAM

Less frequently used than hot water, with which it is often confused. Both hot water and steam use a "boiler." There is no pump. Steam operates on higher temperatures, so the house heats up more quickly than with hot water, but still more slowly than with an air-distribution system. Water vapor escaping into rooms (with some steam systems) can increase winter comfort by raising humidity. Old systems may "knock" or hiss.

RADIANT

My candidate for the most comfortable system, when installed in the form of hot water pipes in the floor; and the worst, most uncomfortable, in the form of electrical resistance coils in the ceiling. Unfortunately, radiant heat pipes in a concrete floor are very expensive to repair if they should leak, as the floor has to be broken up.

BASEBOARD, ELECTRIC

Comfortable and quiet, maintenance-free, and permits individual temperature control in each unit or room if so installed. Expensive to operate except where electricity is cheap.

THE HEAT PUMP

The heat pump is an apparent modern miracle that works like a reversible air conditioning system to move heat either into your house from the outside, or vice-versa, by means of two compressors and a refrigerant line. Remember, there is "heat" in any substance at a temperature above absolute zero (-273.15°C). It is practical and economical both as central heating and air conditioning in parts of the United States where winter temperatures typically do not fall below freezing for much of the time. It is not as efficient as resistance electrical heating in the cold North, unless of the water-to-air type, which can remove heat from copper coils submerged in a well or a pond. Heat pumps installed before 1972 have experienced problems, especially compressor failure. The newer ones have a better maintenance record.

5

"SPACE HEATERS"

In older homes, houses which have been substantially added onto, and in warmer parts of the country where central heating has not always been considered essential, you may find one or another kind of stove designed to heat only one room. A stove or space heater will not ordinarily heat an adjacent room, except in the warmest climates. Electric space heaters, if properly wired and grounded, will generally be safe (although expensive to operate). Gas- or oil-fired heaters may be divided into three groups:

Unvented room heaters These, without a flue to carry away combustion gases, should be rejected. They can release carbon monoxide into the room.

Vented heaters drawing combustion air from inside the room — are safer than the above. They still share with them the drawback of using up the oxygen supply inside a house. A space heater is unsafe in a tightly closed house or room, where it may cause asphyxiation.

Vented, through-the-wall heaters — have a double vent pipe extending horizontally from the stove through the wall, and not only direct their exhaust gases outside, but draw combustion air back through the outer concentric tube. They are safest. With them, you should be concerned that their combustion chamber (like that of any other furnace) is sound, and that their exhaust flue is not located where it may scorch a wooden wall surface or someone passing by outside. Some mortgage institutions will not lend money for the purchase of a house equipped solely with space heaters.

AIR CONDITIONING Central air conditioning works along

the same principle as your refrigerator. The cooling coils are located in the plenum of the furnace. Cool air, instead of warm, is circulated by the furnace blower in the summer, controlled by the same thermostat. Heat from the warm house is picked up at the coil by the refrigerant (a volatile liquid such as Freon) as it expands into a gas in the cooling coils. The gas is then pumped under low pressure to the outside of the house, where the heat is "squeezed" out of it by a compressor and blown away by a fan into the outside air. The refrigerant, now under high pressure, is pumped back to the cooling coil in the plenum to pick up more heat. As the house air is cooled, it loses water, which runs off the cooling coils and out of the furnace plenum by a drip line.

In the West, where the summer air is less humid than in the East, evaporative coolers are frequently used. These are also called "swamp coolers." They use a separate duct system from that of the central furnace. Evaporative coolers are cheaper to install and economical to operate. They simply blow air over pads or screens so that it cools by evaporation. The dampened cool air is then distributed into the house.

ELECTRICAL SYSTEM I am a great partisan of older homes, but I have to admit that one area in which the older home usually suffers by comparison with modern ones is the electrical system. Until the 1930s it was considered adequate for a house to be supplied with fifteen or thirty amperes of current at the meter. Lighting and outlets were stingy by modern standards. Each bedroom would have only one outlet, the bathroom might have none at all, and the kitchen two at most. The entire house would be wired on two or three circuits, protected by fuses that had to be replaced whenever an overload occurred. As more and more electrical appliances came to be used in American homes, some owners began to modify the electrical systems of their older homes, occasionally in dangerous ways. Fuses were used with greater rated strengths than the current that the wiring would safely carry. Extra outlets were "bootlegged" by running lamp cord along the baseboards and up the walls.

The kitchen is one area where the owner of an older house feels the pinch. Where can you plug in an electric fry pan, roaster, waffle iron, microwave oven, and coffee pot, maybe a clock and a radio too? A fifteen ampere circuit (which the older kitchen probably shares with another couple of rooms) will carry only 1800 watts. This means if you plug in a toaster of 1200 watts and a coffeepot of 800 watts simultaneously, you'll blow a fuse.

By contrast, houses built after 1960 will be supplied with both 120 volt and 240 volt current, with a rated capacity at the meter of 100, 150, or even 200 amps. Heavy appliances such as electrical resistance heaters, air conditioners, ranges, garbage disposals, clothes dryers, electrical water heaters, and dishwashers may each be wired into its own separate circuit. Instead of the awkward fuse box, you will probably have a circuit breaker panel with labels to tell you which appliance or section of the house is on which circuit. The kitchen will have two 20 amp, 120 volt circuits for kitchen appliances, and rooms will be provided with an outlet for every twelve feet of wall length.

The electrical systems of many older homes have been updated by their owners. If yours has not, you should consider the cost of eventually doing so when you purchase the house; it will increase your resale price, as well as make life easier and safer.

WATER SUPPLY In most cities and many rural areas you'll never have to give a thought to a water supply that is already piped to the house. Where the water is especially hard, a water softener will be advisable and you may find one already installed. What we call "hard" water, with its attendant problems of decreased effectiveness of hand soaps, a sludge left behind in tubs and basins, with scale build-up in pipes and hot water heaters, is caused primarily by magnesium and calcium compounds dissolved in the water. In some regions of the country the problem is so severe that many water heater manufacturers won't distribute their products, as the predicted life of a water heater is shorter than the length of the guarantee.

The most common treatment to remedy hardness in water is an "ion-exchange" water softener, in which the magnesium and calcium in the water are exchanged for the more active mineral sodium, derived from common salt. Such a water softener may be serviced by a private company, or you may have an installation that automatically back-flushes when its sodium is exhausted. Water softeners put high quantities of sodium in the water, which becomes dangerous to drink for a person with a heart condition. For this reason, water softeners are frequently connected only to the supply of the water heater, to protect it from scale build-up, leaving the cold water in the house untreated.

If your water comes from a well, get a written statement from the owner testifying to the past water supply, the capacity of the well, its output and depth, as well as the performance specifications of the pump. This request will prompt him to tell you the truth about any marginal water supply. You will be able to sue him if he fails to disclose the true situation.

A septic tank is a similar situation. Have the seller furnish a description of the outlet from the house, the distance to the field, together with a map of the drainage field, including the location of the access cover. Ask what the service record has been, and when the tank was last pumped out. You should also ask the neighbors whether they know of any problems with the septic drainage. If you intend to add a bathroom, check with the local health department or building inspection division before you buy the house, to be sure that the existing tank and field are large enough.

INSULATION In the good old days of cheap energy, home insulation received little attention. Now it has become a subject of major importance. You should expect insulation in the walls of frame houses, in the attic, and under floors over unheated crawl spaces. The solid, double brick, masonry walls of our finest old homes are, unfortunately, good conductors of heat. Timber frame houses faced with brick have a single layer of bricks with an air space between it and the plaster or sheetrock wall inside. In recent houses this air space may be filled with insulation. Even without insulation, the air space is a better barrier to heat flow than solid masonry. All-electric and solar-heated homes must be more carefully insulated than ordinary ones.

As important as good insulation, but often neglected, although cheap to install, is effective weatherstripping and caulking around windows, doors, and trim.

Double-glazed windows and storm doors are a great advantage. They will reduce heat loss at these vulnerable areas by half. Only in the mildest climate does a house with many windows and glass doors make sense, from an energy-conscious point of view.

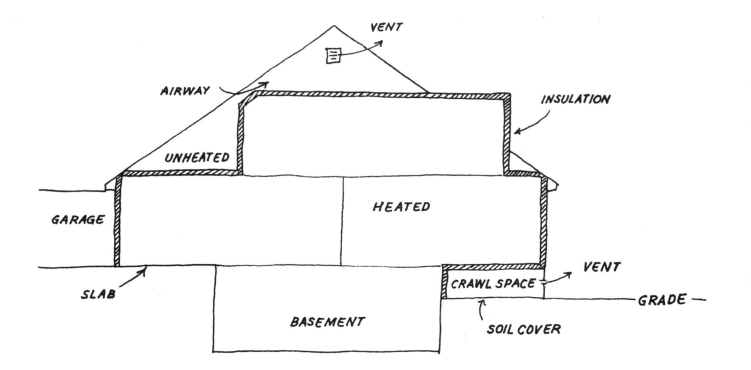

Placement of insulation

CONDOMINIUMS Most of the advice in this book applies to the buyer of a condominium as well as to the buyer of a house. A condominium entails the purchase of a specified portion of a building, together with the right to use certain common areas and services. You must pay for the continuing upkeep of these common facilities. A condominium is more than a dwelling unit; it is also a legal obligation. You should inspect your condominium agreement as carefully as the heating and the plumbing.

Examine carefully the estimate of continuing maintenance and management costs for the homeowners association. Watch out for unrealistically low estimates that entice you to buy, and which can be increased later.

Is the management contract between the homeowners association and the managing company breakable? If not, you will have no protection against unreasonable and unlimited increases in management charges.

Are the bylaws and agreements in the homeowners association contract carefully written? Do they spell out clearly which questions are subject to direct vote by all members, and which can be decided by the board of directors alone?

Does your contract clearly indicate which repairs are to be paid by the association, and which by the individual?

Is the contract clear on such issues as whether particular parking spaces are assigned to a particular unit, which elements are private, which are used in common, and which are "limited common elements" (owned in common but assigned to a particular individual)?

Are there restraints as to whom you may in turn sell the unit?

Inspect all the various parts of the building, such as stairs, elevators, heating plant, and roof, which serve your unit and which are held in common, for which you may be assessed when repairs are needed. If possible, estimate their life expectancy before repairs may be needed.

BEFORE YOU BEGIN

As you look over the houses or condominiums which are for sale in the area which you have chosen, good design and space adequate for your needs will be your dominant concerns. As your choice narrows to one in particular, its physical condition — how well it has been cared for

11

by previous owners — comes to the fore. The remaining chapters in this book are your guide to careful inspection. Through them runs an overriding concern, to which your attention will repeatedly be drawn, and that is the problem of water damage.

Water is the chief enemy of any house. Keep a sound roof on a structure and it may last hundreds of years. Let the water leak in and it will be destroyed. Not only is a house threatened by a faulty roof, but by poor peripheral drainage, ground water rising in the basement, broken supply lines, poorly sealed tub and shower enclosures, corroded drains, leaking appliances and hot water heating systems. Water can do horrible things to a house. It can bring down plaster ceilings, skew foundations, warp floors, and foster dry rot. But don't panic. None of the ravages of water occur without leaving visible signs. I always approach an inspection by assuming that the property is a disaster area, thinly papered over, and make it prove itself otherwise. Open your eyes and follow the instructions, which will repeatedly direct you to look for water damage that may appear in many different places.

CHAPTER TWO: ON THE JOB

Don't try to inspect a house the first time you see it. Let your mind consider the larger questions of whether you find the house attractive, large enough, and at a price you can afford. Does the location suit you? Is it near schools, work, shopping, bus lines? Does the house have the features you want? Is the yard attractive? Unless the answers to these questions are affirmative, you won't be inspecting it anyway.

When you find a house for the right price with the proper location and features you need, then sit down with the realtor—or the owner, if you aren't buying through a realtor—and draw up a contract. This is your offer to buy the house at a certain price. Now is the time to insist that the following clause be inserted into the contract:

"This contract to buy is subject to buyer or his agents' satisfactory inspection of heating, plumbing, electrical wiring, roof, structure, and general condition of the property, including house and garage (if any).

Said inspection shall be completed within seven days of approval of this contract by seller, and may include subsequent inspection for termites or by whatever experts buyer may consider necessary. Any such subsequent inspection shall be concluded not later than ten days from the date of approval of this contract by seller.''

Once the seller has approved your offer, you should get ready to inspect the house. First, make an appointment for the inspection. Choose a time early enough in the day so that you will have three hours to finish before dark. It shouldn't take that long, but if you're late starting or run into unexpected puzzles, you don't want to be forced to hurry. The owner needn't be present at the time, but he (or she) will be an asset to learning about the property, so you want to include him if convenient. The realtor will want to meet you at the house to let you in and accompany you on the inspection.

When you make the appointment, remind the realtor to have all the utilities turned on. Especially when a house is vacant, the precaution may be necessary: you can't inspect plumbing if the water's turned off—not to mention wiring and heating if there's no gas or electricity. Even in an occupied house, the furnace pilot may be shut off during the summer. Ask to be given access to all storerooms, parts of the basement, garage, etc., that might be locked.

Wear work clothes or coveralls on the inspection so you won't hesitate to enter a crawl space or get dirty, if necessary, in an attic. Wear shoes with non-skid soles if you will be climbing onto the roof. You'll need a set of simple tools. Borrow these if you don't have them already, or buy them at the neighborhood hardware store (a good place to ask questions about typical area problems). The largest item is a five-foot stepladder. You may ask the owner if he has one you can use. You'll need the ladder to reach the attic unless there is a finished stairway.

Your second tool is a good flashlight. A standard one, powered by two "D" cells, will be bright enough if the batteries are fresh. Even better is the larger flashlight which uses a 6-volt dry cell. One of these in an unlighted crawl space is almost as good as a 100-watt bulb. You will need a standard flat-bladed screwdriver of medium size, a packet of matches (in case you have to light a pilot flame), a red pen and a black pen, and an electrical circuit tester. The latter can be found at a hardware store for about $1.00. The simplest kind has two insulated probes about five inches long, with a bulb, and is suitable for testing 120v and 240v current. If the house is equipped with a warm air furnace fueled by natural gas or propane, purchase a small bottle of oil of wintergreen and a cheap artist's brush at a drug store. To inspect a steep roof which you can see, but don't want to climb onto, a pair of binoculars will be handy. Lastly, bring litmus paper if you want to check the acidity of a solar collector system protected by ethylene gylcol anti-freeze.

So much for your tools. Equally important is the state of mind for the kind of detective work you'll be doing. Obviously it comes more easily when you're familiar with what you're doing. Go through a "dress rehearsal," a practice inspection, at a friend's house or where you are presently living. Take your flashlight and follow the directions in this book, beginning with the basement and proceeding through the interior, the attic, to the roof and outside. Mark the check sheets lightly in pencil as you go along. Erase these marks completely before your real inspection. Use the illustrations in this book to help you identify the parts of a house you may not recognize, like the framing, the furnace controls, the drain clean-out plugs. Train your eyes to look at a ceiling carefully for signs of a leak, or to examine a chimney for loose bricks.

The day of the inspection has come. Is it scheduled for afternoon, with a busy morning first? Then give yourself time over a leisurely lunch to relax. Don't rush into an inspection with other things on your mind. If you're inclined to be sleepy, drink a cup of coffee.

Protect your ability to concentrate while you're on the job. The realtor may want to be chatty; the owner, to brag about his beautiful house. Both are inclined to follow you around, looking over your shoulder and making conversation about the state of the economy or yesterday's ball game. Explain to them politely that you must concentrate on the inspection, but you will also need them handy to answer questions. Perhaps they wouldn't mind waiting in the living room where you can find them?

Look over the house from the outside before entering. Examine the lines of the roof ridge and the eaves. Do they dip or sag? If so, some structural trouble is indicated, either uneven foundation settlement or failure of framing timbers. Make a note on the attic check sheet to inspect this area carefully from the inside later on. Now examine the corners of the house itself, perhaps sighting along them to another vertical line such as a utility pole or another house. Does the corner

15

show any lean or unevenness? Are there cracks noticeable near the corners of the wall or in the foundation walls? Are sidewalks or porches badly cracked or dislocated? If you notice any of these signs, the house misalignment may be caused by foundation problems. Make a note to inspect the basement or crawl space with extra care.

Before entering the house, take a moment to consider the general condition of the exterior and the yard. Are there obvious problems which you notice at first glance, such as missing screens, cracked windowpanes, leaking gutters, peeling paint, and broken steps? A euphemism for a house in poor condition is "deferred maintenance." This means that the owner has not repaired, or has repaired badly and by cheap, temporary means, the defects of his house. Maybe he said to himself, "Why make an expensive repair when I'm only going to sell the house, anyway?" As a rule, if people don't fix one obvious thing, they won't have fixed the less obvious things either, so look carefully. When you spot that first rusted vent, broken window or leaking pipe, double your vigilance. The chances are that you'll find more problems that need attention.

If you buy a house with "deferred maintenance," you can depend on having to fix one thing after another for months or years. If you're saving a lot of money on the purchase price, or if you're handy with tools and don't mind the extra work, such repairs may be acceptable. But if you expected a trouble-free home, correcting all the problems in a long-neglected house will be a discouraging experience. So go into the purchase with your eyes open by reading the next six chapters and following the procedures carefully.

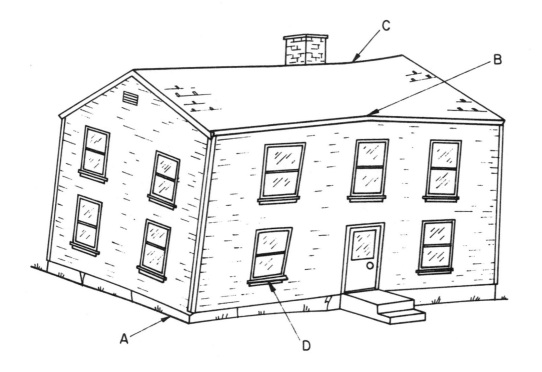

Evidence of uneven foundation settlement may include
(A) house badly out of square,
(B) eave line distortion,
(C) sagging roof ridge,
(D) loose-fitting or binding windows or doors.

(Source: Forest Products Laboratory, Forest Service, USDA)

**THE
HOME
INSPECTION
WORKBOOK**

18

CHAPTER THREE: THE BASEMENT AND CRAWL SPACE

Some of the most serious, the most elusive, and the most difficult to repair of all housing problems originate in the basement. It is usually the most neglected part of any house and, for the inexperienced inspector, the most confusing, filled as it may be with furnace, water heater, plumbing, vents, hot and cold air runs, loose wiring, structural timbers, and the accumulated junk of half a century. Here, perhaps more than in any other part of the house, it is important to go slowly and methodically to look for signs of every possible defect. In this chapter we shall examine the various aspects of the structure of the house as they may be viewed from the basement or crawl space. In Chapter Four we will have a look at furnace, hot water heater, plumbing, and wiring. For now, do not think about these mechanical systems.

DAMPNESS The first thing you should do upon entering the basement or crawl space is to inspect for dampness. Immediately upon opening the door or stepping into the basement, sniff the air critically. Is it musty, or dry and clean? There are many possible causes of dampness in a basement, only one of which is difficult or impossible to cure. The most frequent source of water entering a basement is from the surface. A carelessly placed lawn sprinkler can spray an outside wall surface and flood the basement. More common are defective downspouts or gutters, or poor slope of the ground around the building. We will deal with these problems and how to remedy them in Chapter Nine, "The Weather Side." Another origin of the water can be from within the house itself: a leaking water line or a clogged or broken drain, for example. If you detect dampness and eliminate all of the above sources, its origin may be either condensation or ground water. In summertime it is common for moisture in the warm air to condense on the cool basement walls and water pipes. It may drip from these onto floors and supports. These problems may be alleviated by improved ventilation or by insulating the walls and wrapping the pipes to prevent condensation.

A much more serious problem is a high water table in the ground beneath the house which forces water into the basement. If this manifests itself as nothing more than damp walls after a rainy spell, you may be able to cure them by painting the inside with a water sealant or a coat of cement. Before you do this, be certain the ground slope around the house is correct! But if water periodically rises up in a flood, you can attempt to prevent it by ditching and installing a drain below basement level all around the house, and by sealing the basement walls from the outside. Even these measures don't infallibly work. The reason to consider a damp basement a serious menace is that high humidity provides a favorable environment for the growth of decay fungus and insect pests, which will cheerfully devour your house from beneath.

Having sniffed the air to detect any damp or musty odor, switch on all the lights and look around. If you find the basement floor littered with trunks, boxes of old clothes, furniture, and the like, you can be reasonably sure to have discovered a dry basement. If such things are not present, inspect the condition of the baseboard or other wood near floor level. Is it soft, discolored, or stained? Is rust present on the heads of nails? Inspect the furnace frame or other iron objects near floor level (but not the water heater, which is subject to its own rust problems) for corrosion which might be due to water. Examine the condition of the floor itself. A dirt floor will reveal the periodic presence of water: either mud, dried mud, or channels will be evident. Water entering through a concrete floor will leave cracks, stains, and mineral deposits leached from the concrete itself.

Is the floor buckled or humped? These may be signs of ground water or of unstable subsoil. Linoleum or asphalt tile laid on concrete will curl at the corners or warp in the presence of water, and a white deposit will remain around the tiles. A wooden floor which has periodically been wet will be damp, soft from decay, springy (if termites are present), or bleached and rough. If you detect signs of periodic dampness, enter your observations in red on the check sheet and try to locate the origin of the water. If you don't find that the water has entered through the basement walls or windows, or has originated in the house itself (such as from a leaking water pipe or the roof), make a note to ask the owner about the water problem in the basement, and perhaps ask the neighbors, too, whether there has been occasional flooding or a high water table.

FOUNDATION Now direct your attention to the foundation walls. You must gain access to any crawl spaces or storage areas which permit you to inspect the entire perimeter of the foundation from the inside. If there seems to be no access to some area, ask the owner why not. With his permission, pry open and look inside any closed area. As you go along with your flashlight, keep your eyes open for four things: 1) cracks, and in the case of masonry walls, missing mortar; 2) stains indicating water entry; 3) any wood in contact with the ground, which you will probe for hardness; 4) pencil-sized or slightly larger earthen tubes from the ground leading to wood, which are the sheltered runways of termites.

Almost any concrete foundation wall will have some fine cracks in it. These are usually due to temperature changes, minor uneven settlement, or shrinkage of the concrete when setting. The cracks you are concerned about are large open cracks, especially ones that run vertically or diagonally and are wider at top than bottom. Such cracks are caused by uneven settling of the foundation, and must be considered

21

Ceiling damage caused by foundation shift due to swelling soil

Heaved concrete slab from soil swelling

(Source: Stephen S. Hart, Colorado Department of Natural Resources)

BASEMENT AND CRAWL SPACE

Crack in wall caused by foundation movement
(Source: Stephen S. Hart, Colorado Department of Natural Resources)

23

to be more serious in a new or recent house than in an old one, where it is more likely that the rate of settling has slowed down or stopped. In a foundation wall of brick or block, cracks which run right across the bricks are more serious than ones which follow the mortar joints. Make a note on the check sheet in red if you find any serious cracks, or a great many small ones. We'll consider them again in the section on evaluation.

Note, also, if the mortar is soft between bricks, or missing altogether. Where the wall is very old (fifty or more years) and otherwise stable, the mortar may not have been very good to begin with and has simply crumbled with age. You can replace it. In a newer wall, the absence of mortar will suggest water entry. Large blisters on a plaster surface indicate dampness in the wall behind.

Wherever you see indications of water stains, make a note to inspect the location outside the house at the end of the inspection. If it corresponds with a low spot, defective gutter, or downspout, the water can probably be diverted easily, or the low spot filled with earth. Sometimes a bad water stain can result from a carelessly placed sprinkler.

DECAY AND INSECT DAMAGE
Every time you encounter wood within six inches of the earth, inspect it for softness or decay. Likely places are windowsills or framing members like posts, girders, joists, or stairs, door frames, and the like. Visual signs of decay are a loss of natural sheen and either a darkening or bleaching accompanied by fine black lines in the wood along the grain. The presence of fuzzy strands, fibrous or mushroomlike growths is a giveaway that the wood has been attacked by fungus. So-called dry rot occurs in the presence of high humidity, like all other forms of decay, and leaves the affected wood dark brown and crumbly to the touch. Probe with your screwdriver. You should not be able to push the blade more than ¼ inch into sound wood. Pry with the blade of the screwdriver; sound wood will break into sharp splinters, whereas wood that is rotten will crumble or check, breaking away into rectangular pieces.

Occasionally one comes across framing timbers, joists, or plywood with a whitewash on the surface that is powdery to the touch. If this is a fine layer of dried cement, don't worry: it only means that the contractor economized by using the same wood for framing which he used to build the forms for the concrete foundation walls.

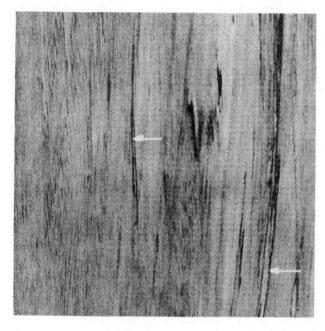

Bleached appearance of decayed wood accompanied by appearance of fine black lines along the grain

(Source: Forest Products Laboratory, Forest Service, USDA)

(A) termite in winged stage,
(B) flying ant, showing narrow waist

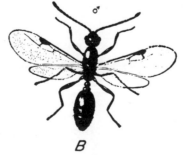

(Source: Forest Products Laboratory, Forest Service, USDA)

Fungus growth in damp crawl space under joist. Pen shows comparative size.

(Source: Forest Products Laboratory, Forest Service, USDA)

Advanced decay in wood, showing cubical checking and collapse

TERMITES

Several varieties of insects will attack wood in a house. Among these, the termite is the most serious and generates a fear entirely out of proportion to the damage it usually causes. There are two principal types of termites: the dry-wood termites, common in the tropics and found (in the U.S.A.) chiefly in Hawaii, Southern California, the Gulf Coast, and Florida, that fly directly to and bore into wood instead of building tunnels from the ground. They carve chambers across the grain of the wood. They do not require access to water, but remain hidden in the wood until they mature, grow wings, and emerge to fly away to new locations. You may be able to detect the excrement of these termites in the form of sandlike pellets discarded outside the wood.

Subterranean termites, government experts tell us, "are common throughout the eastern half of the United States and along the Pacific Coast. They are abundant from Massachusetts south along the Atlantic Coast and along the Gulf of Mexico, in the Ohio River Valley, in the southern part of the Missouri and Mississippi river valleys, and in Southern California."[1] (See the map.) They become relatively unimportant at the northern limits of their range. Subterranean termites eat long galleries along the grain of the wood they inhabit, but leave the surface untouched. A house timber can be tunneled out from inside with very little evidence on the surface (paint will frequently blister or peel away from such a surface, however, as it will from mildewed or decayed wood). As they must have contact with water to survive, and their most dependable source is in the earth, these termites may reveal their presence by earthen corridors about ¼ - ½ inch wide that they construct across foundation walls or along pipes from the earth to wood. A substantial crack in the foundation may give them concealed access, or they may enter a house where careless construction has left wood in contact with the soil.

Where termites are present, exterminators can inject the timbers and the soil under and around the house with poison which will kill them and prevent their reappearance for a long time. The important thing is to discover them. Look for their earthen runways in the shape of flattened tubes. Probe carefully wherever you find wood close to or in contact with the soil. Look for dead insects (¼ inch long) or their discarded wings (½ inch) on the inside of basement windowsills.

---

1. L. O. Anderson and O. C. Heyer, *Wood Frame House Construction*, U. S. Department of Agriculture (Washington, D.C., 1955), p. 197.

A *The northern limit of damage (in the United States) by subterranean termites.*
B *The northern limit of damage by dry-wood or nonsubterranean termites.*

(Source: Forest Products Laboratory, Forest Service, USDA)

Many varieties of ants live in houses. They also have a flying stage. Ants can be distinguished from termites by their slender waists; hard, shiny bodies; and dark color. Termites have longer wings, proportionately, and are characteristic of uniform thickness from head to tail, without a "waist." They are soft-bodied and pale in color (although some flying forms may be darker). If you have any reason to suspect termites, ask the owner to give you a guarantee that the structure is free of them and will remain so for one year.

CARPENTER ANTS

Only one variety of ant actually nests within the wood of a house: carpenter ants. They do not actually eat the wood, but merely excavate a nest in it, depositing the chewed wood outside in piles of sawdust. An appropriate insecticide will kill them if sprayed into the nest. Eliminate moisture in the area to discourage them.

POWDER POST BEETLES

A number of beetles will bore into dead wood, including the timbers of a house. The most serious pests among these are the "death-watch beetles" (anobiids), which make a distinctive clicking sound, and the more destructive, smaller, powder post beetles (lyctids). These will even bore into furniture and tool handles, leaving behind a packed powder the consistency of flour. Adult powder post beetles are 1–7 mm (1/25"–1/4") long, reddish-brown to black in color. They leave the wood through a hole about the thickness of a pencil lead, which can give the wood an appearance of having been hit by birdshot. Like other beetles, the adults carry their wings under hard shells (wing cases). The larva are soft-bodied weevils. Powder post beetles, found in humid locations, are a pest chiefly in the eastern and southern regions of the United States.

BEES

If you find a substantial round hole perhaps 3/8"–1/2" in diameter on the outside of your house, you may be startled by the sudden emergence of a large carpenter bee. Don't worry. These bees do not eat wood, but only tunnel a small nest. And they are solitary, not colonial like ants and honeybees. Unless you live near a forest, you probably won't see very many of them. Wild honeybees can be more of a problem. Again, they do not eat wood, or even tunnel into it, but, finding a hole in your wall or attic window, a hive may establish itself in your house and defy efforts to remove it.

VENTILATION Wood-boring insects generally avoid wood that is thoroughly dry. This is the reason good basement or crawl space ventilation is important. The average basement with finished floor, windows, and access to the house above will probably receive enough ventilation. Where earth is exposed under a house, however, a vapor barrier (commonly a black plastic sheet or tar paper) over the soil is recommended, and ventilation is essential. Crawl spaces may be vented either to the outside or to a partial basement, if there is one. The vents must have a total free area of at least 1/150 of the floor area where the soil is not covered by a vapor barrier. Where a moisture-proof barrier is laid over the soil, the vents need be no more than 1/1500 of the ground area. Vents to the outside are best located on opposite sides of the house to ensure cross-ventilation.

If your house has a crawl space instead of a basement, and is vented to the outside, you will want to have under-the-floor insulation in all but the warmest parts of the country. This insulation should be 3"-4" thick and faced with a vapor barrier or foil on the top, or warm side, against the floor. All pipes and heating ducts, including cold-air returns, should likewise be insulated with 2 inches of fiberglass wrap (foil on the outside). Insulation only on the outside walls, around the perimeter of the crawl space, is not much use if the crawl space is provided with ventilation so that cold air will enter.

A full basement will not require below-floor insulation, but you may want to insulate the foundation walls if they are of concrete or brick. Concrete block, with its many air cells, is rather a good insulator by itself. Check on the inspection sheet if any insulation is present.

FRAMING AND SUBFLOOR Direct your attention to the house framing—what's holding up the floor above your head. A small house may have joists running entirely across from one foundation wall to the other. More commonly these joists, upon which the subfloor is directly laid, are themselves supported by beams (of wood), a girder (perhaps of steel), or a masonry-bearing wall perpendicular to the joists. A steel girder or wooden beams will be supported in their turn by posts of wood or steel, or, in older homes, by brick columns. Inspect each of these. A brick column should not be crumbly or leaning. A post should be vertical and free from rot or termites at the bottom; it should rest on a concrete pier, not directly on the earth. Beams and joists should not sag at their centers enough to be discernible to the eye. If they sag at one end, it is an indication of foundation settlement or failure. The floor above will slope toward that side of the house. (Make a note to inspect this floor from above and to look at the outside of the house for more indications of settlement.)

How thick are the joists, how far apart, and how long do they run between supports? If they are 2″ x 8″ (actually 1½″ x 7¼″) on sixteen-inch centers, and do not span more than twelve feet between supports, they should be firm enough. A nominal 2″ x 10″ (actually 1½″ by 9¼″) can span fourteen feet comfortably. If the joists are undersized (such as 2″ x 6″), or span too great a length, the floor above may be weak or springy. It will be likely that the builder may have skimped in other less obvious places.

In a finished basement the joists will be covered up by a basement ceiling and none of the house-framing may be visible. In that case you will just have to do the best you can, looking into closets and other areas to find an open ceiling where you can form some opinion of the size and condition of the floor joists above you. At least you can carefully examine the ceilings and tops of partition walls for signs of cracks and failure. These partition walls can be a problem in areas threatened by swelling soils. There, the proper design for such walls requires that they be "floated," or hung from the ceiling, so that any rise in the basement floor caused by swelling soil will not warp or displace the floor above. It's often difficult to tell by visual inspection whether a partition wall has been "floated." Ask the owner whether partition walls are part of the original construction, and if not, whether he installed them or had them built. If he built them, did he float them or instruct his builder to do so? If he didn't have them floated, or doesn't know what the term means, these partition walls could cause you trouble if the soil beneath the basement floor should swell.

Where there is no finished ceiling in a basement, you will be able to see the subfloor (not the finished floor) resting on the joists. The subfloor is usually of 1-inch or ¾-inch pine or fir planks laid diagonally

31

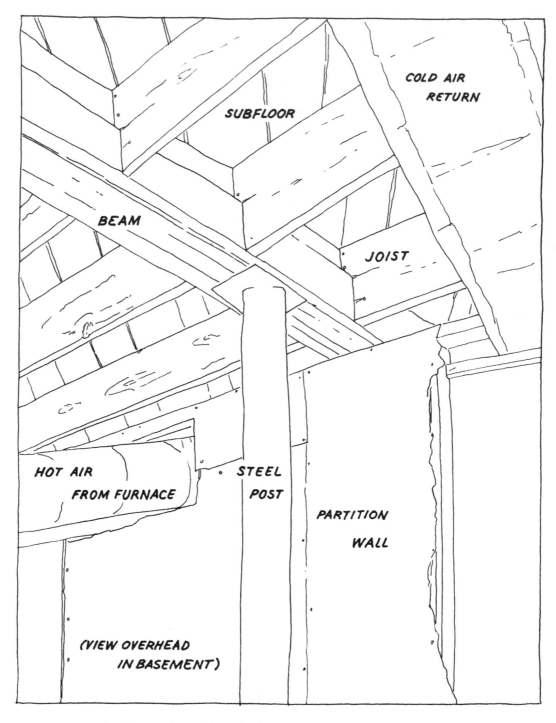

Subfloor and framing as viewed from the basement

to the joists for greater rigidity. In more recent houses it is usually 5/8-inch or thicker plywood. With your flashlight, examine all areas where the subfloor is visible; watch for dampness, or discoloration that might be a sign of past dampness. Look closely around pipes that pass through the subfloor: here may be the best place to tell what leaks exist in the kitchen or bathroom plumbing above. Sinks, tub, and shower overhead are indicated by paired hot and cold lines. The toilet waste line (also called the soil line) has a diameter of 4 inches and is a frequent source of trouble. If the wood around any of the pipes or drains is discolored or has white encrustations indicating either mineral accumulation or fungus growth, probe with the screwdriver to see if the wood is soft. If so, it must be replaced.

Where you find dampness, or suspect recent dampness, return to this spot after running the water in the fixtures above. Identify the source of the leak, if any, and inform the owner of the house that you expect it to be fixed, or the price of the house to be reduced accordingly, before you buy it. (Record any such conditions in red on the check sheet.)

While inspecting the subfloor, keep your eyes open for anything else unusual, such as soot or charred wood above the furnace and hot water heater. Either of these is an indication of a dangerous condition in these appliances, unless it has already been repaired or adjusted.

BASEMENT CHECK SHEET

EVIDENCE OF MOISTURE: on floor _____ walls _____ other _____ none _____

FLOOR: concrete _____ other _____ condition, good _____ fair _____
poor _____ cracked _____ badly cracked _____ heaved _____

WALLS: concrete _____ block _____ brick _____ plaster _____ other _____
cracks _____ mortar missing _____

DECAY OR INSECT DAMAGE: yes _____ not visible _____
location _____

VENTILATION: adequate _____ not adequate _____

INSULATION: under floor _____ on walls _____ on pipes _____
none _____ vapor barrier present _____

COLUMNS: steel _____ wood _____ masonry _____ other _____
not visible _____ condition, good _____ poor _____

GIRDERS: steel _____ wood _____ none _____ not visible _____
condition, good _____ poor _____

FLOOR JOISTS: size and spacing _____ condition, good _____
poor _____ not visible _____

SUBFLOOR: planks _____ plywood _____ condition, good _____ poor _____
not visible _____ leak _____

OBSERVATIONS:_____

_____

SEE BACK OF BOOK FOR DETACHABLE CHECK SHEETS

CHAPTER FOUR: OPERATING SYSTEMS

INSPECTING THE CENTRAL HEATING SYSTEM[1]

Locate the metal tag on the furnace which describes its capacity, its fuel supply, etc. You may find it inside an access panel that you will have to remove. Look to see whether the tag has a date of manufacture stamped on it; if not, perhaps a careful owner has kept a service record near the furnace. This is a valuable source of information as to its age and condition.

In a moderate climate, a normal house, well insulated, requires a furnace of fifty BTU/hr. input capacity per square foot of floor area. Irregularly shaped houses, poorly insulated houses, or houses in colder climates require more heat: for the Rocky Mountains and the northern Great Plains, 80 BTU/hr. per square foot would not be too much, and perhaps 100 BTU/hr. per square foot is advisable in Montana and Minnesota. Multiply the area of your house by the appropriate figure.

---

[1] If your house does not have a central heating system, it may be heated by electric baseboard heat or wall furnaces. Where you have these or other independently controlled space heaters, check them in each room as you inspect the house. Be sure they will heat all the rooms evenly and adequately.

For example, a 1600-square-foot house in Washington, D.C., might require a furnace rated at 80,000 BTU/hr. input, while the same house in Chicago or Denver should be equipped with one of 128,000 BTU/hr. input capacity. This illustration is only a rough estimate.

Forced-air furnaces cannot operate beyond their rated capacity. Hot water or steam boilers will, so their ratings are less critical. Electric furnaces, because they do not lose heat up the chimney, may be adequate at lower-rated capacities, calculated in kilowatt hours (1 Kh = 3410 BTU/hr.). Seventeen Kh or 58,000 BTU/hr. may be sufficient for an electric furnace to heat our hypothetical three-bedroom Washington, D.C., house. Remember, any electrically heated house should be heavily insulated.

If your house has had one or more rooms added to the original structure, find out whether the addition has its own source of heat or whether it depends on the central furnace. If the furnace is the one installed in the original house, does it have the capacity to heat the addition as well? Has the duct work been tapped into for the addition, or (in the case of hot water or steam) have additional radiators been added? A large addition, if properly done, will require either its own separate furnace or a new furnace large enough to serve both the original house and the addition. When you turn on the furnace, following the procedures outlined below, run it long enough to be certain that both the addition and the original portion of the house are receiving adequate heat.

No flammables should be stored next to a furnace, and the immediate area around it should be kept free from clutter. If the furnace is located in a small room, it will require an opening to the outside to provide combustion air. A furnace that sits in the middle of an open basement will probably get enough combustion air from the rest of the house, through leaks around windows and doors. Modern well-sealed houses with poured concrete foundations can allow so little outside air to enter that you may have to open a window to allow the furnace to burn properly. Ideally, the furnace room should be fitted with a fire-resistant door; this is especially important in a small furnace room. Galvanized steel, 5/8-inch sheetrock, or asbestos backing on an ordinary door is acceptable.

All furnaces other than electric have a flue or chimney to carry away waste gases. Examine this carefully for signs of cracks, separation, or

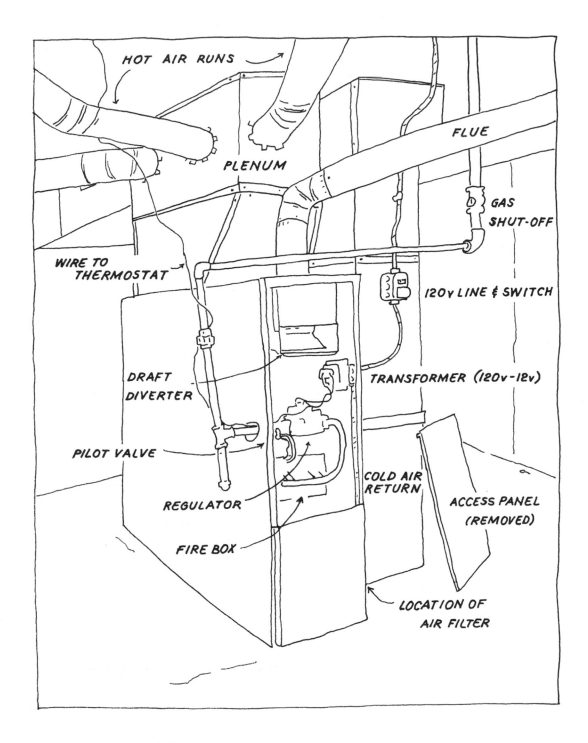

HOT AIR RUNS

FLUE

PLENUM

GAS SHUT-OFF

WIRE TO THERMOSTAT

120v LINE & SWITCH

DRAFT DIVERTER

TRANSFORMER (120v-12v)

PILOT VALVE

COLD AIR RETURN

ACCESS PANEL (REMOVED)

REGULATOR

FIRE BOX

LOCATION OF AIR FILTER

Natural gas, forced-air furnace

37

holes. There will be an opening at the base of the flue where it leaves the furnace — this is a draft diverter. The flue must slope upward slightly (at least ¼ inch per foot of horizontal run) from the furnace to the chimney, where it must seal tightly.

A hot water or steam boiler should have no water on it, under it, or discharging from it during operation. If you do find water under such circumstances, make a note in red pen on the check sheet.

Any natural-gas-fired unit must have a safety pilot that will shut off the gas if the pilot flame goes out. You can identify this as a sensing unit in the pilot flame, connected to a valve on the gas line by a set of wires or a thin aluminum tube. Any modern gas furnace will be so equipped; the older furnaces are dangerous if not fitted with this safety pilot.

To inspect the firebox, first make sure the house thermostat (probably located on the main floor in the living room or a hall) is turned down. Open the firebox and shine your flashlight inside. If you're lucky enough to find a furnace with a large firebox door, you will be able to see the top, which is the underside of the heat exchanger. In a newer furnace, the heat exchanger may consist of a number of tubes arranged vertically in the firebox. Are the walls, top, or heat exchanger tubes rusty or cracked? Is there any sign of a leak (in a water system or steam)?

With a gas-fired, air-circulating (forced-air or gravity) furnace, here's a test you can employ to determine whether the heat exchanger is cracked or leaking combustion products into the circulated air. (In an oil or coal furnace the smell of the fuel itself would reveal this defect.) Paint or spray oil of wintergreen onto the sides of the firebox where it will be heated, but not burned, by the flame. When you've turned on the furnace and completed the observation of the functions as described immediately below, let it run and check all the registers in the house for the odor of the wintergreen oil. If you smell it in the warm air flow, you will suspect a cracked heat exchanger. Make a note to call a heating contractor to verify your suspicion with further tests.

With all furnaces, close the firebox door and turn up the thermostat higher than the room temperature. At the furnace, observe the following functions:

1) Feed of fuel into the furnace: with oil, the pressure gun or pump turns on; with coal, the stoker motor runs; with gas, the automatic valve opens.

2) Ignition of burner — is the color of the flame predominantly blue? If much yellow shows, the burner requires adjustment.

3) After a short delay, the circulating motor (pump or blower) switches on; listen for noisy operation — squeaks, rattles, or thumping — that would indicate a worn belt or bearing. It's normal for the burner to ignite and shut off periodically while the fan or pump continues to operate. This cycle is controlled by the high-temperature-limit switch.

Make sure the registers, grilles, or radiators heat up evenly before you turn the thermostat down. Leave a hot water or steam system running long enough to give the radiators time to heat up, completing your inspection of the house in the meantime.

HUMIDIFIER

On a forced-air furnace you may see a humidifier, which should be located on the hot air run at the side or above the furnace. This unit may be identified by labels or instruction tags, and will be connected to a cold water line by a thin copper tube. Humidifiers are often neglected and not repaired when they break down. Check to see if yours is working, once the furnace is operating, by removing access or inspection panels on the unit and ascertaining whether the pads are wet and moving parts are operating. Be careful not to touch any exposed wiring.

CENTRAL AIR CONDITIONER

Inspect a central air conditioner which is integrated with a forced-air furnace by turning down the thermostat to a setting lower than the room temperature. (Undertake this test only when the outdoor temperature is above freezing and the condenser is uncovered.) At the furnace, you should hear the blower operating; the registers that shortly before were blowing warm air will be blowing cold air within a minute or two. The condenser (usually outside, but occasionally found in the attic) will be exhausting warm air.

In a building with a hot water central heating system, an air conditioner will have either its own ductwork for circulating cooled air (in which case the inspection procedure is basically the same as above), or a refrigeration unit to cool the circulating water in the heating system.

Usually installed in larger buildings and apartment complexes, such a refrigeration system should not be turned on when the circulating water is hot. Call a specialist to inspect the unit during cold weather.

PLUMBING Have the seller show you the location of all water shut-off valves, including the main shut-off to the house and those to outside faucets, as well as all drain clean-out plugs. A basement or crawl space is often a confusing maze of criss-crossed pipes, intersected by electrical wires and timbers. Take your time. Shine your flashlight on one pipe after another, following it from floor below to ceiling overhead, until you understand its function and relationship to the other plumbing fixtures. Examine each one carefully to see whether it is leaking at any point, rusty, streaked by water, or repaired. Supply lines (containing water under pressure) are almost always less than an inch in diameter (½ inch or ¾ inch inside), made of galvanized steel or copper pipe. You may also find white plastic (PVC) and lead supply lines. Drains are larger, 1¼ inch to 6 inches in diameter, and are of black cast iron with characteristic hubs (see illustration), copper, steel, black plastic (ABS), or lead.

Among the repairs you may find are small plugs screwed into holes in the lines, or clamshell-like gaskets clamped over a drain or supply line. These repairs are solid, but indicate that the pipe in question is old and will probably leak again somewhere else. Other repairs such as rags, wire, electrical tape, and putty (including epoxy putty) are suitable only for emergencies and are giveaways that the plumbing is in poor condition and has received stingy maintenance. Look for leaks and water on the floor wherever you see corrosion on a supply line. Water does not remain in a drain, of course, so when you see suspicious water marks on a drain, go upstairs and run water into the sink, tub, or toilet that is connected to the drain, then quickly return to the site of the suspected leak and examine it for moisture.

Wherever you find a plumber's "snake" or other drain-cleaning tool, including a can of drain cleaner, you may well imagine the owner has been having problems with a clogged drain. Run water into any basement sink or washtub long enough to be sure the main drain is flowing smoothly.

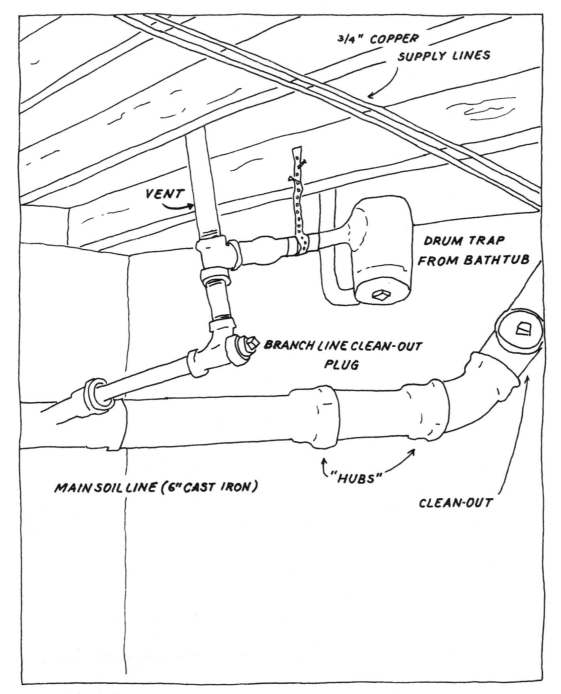

3/4" COPPER SUPPLY LINES

VENT

DRUM TRAP FROM BATHTUB

BRANCH LINE CLEAN-OUT PLUG

MAIN SOIL LINE (6" CAST IRON)

"HUBS"

CLEAN-OUT

Drains, viewed from basement

THE HOME INSPECTION WORKBOOK

THE HOT WATER HEATER

Find the manufacturer's tag. The serial number may have the date of manufacture coded into it, or the plumber who installed it may have left an installation record. The average life of a good water heater should be fifteen to twenty years, but in an area of very hard water it might be only five. The manufacturer's tag will tell you the capacity of the unit and its recovery rate. In a gas or oil hot water heater, 30-gallon storage capacity ought to be sufficient for a family of two or three, 40-gallon for four, 50-gallon for five. Electric hot water heaters have a slow recovery rate and therefore rely on much greater storage capacity. An 80-gallon electric will have the usefulness of a 50-gallon gas water heater. It will have no flue or burner to check. Look for rust on the fittings, water on or underneath the unit, and listen for suspicious noises when it is heating up.

There are many indications of age or wearing out in a gas or oil water heater:

1) Open the firebox door and shine your flashlight into the firebox. Look around the jacket and burner for evidence of moisture or trails of corrosion, which indicate a leaking tank. Moisture can drip down from leaking fittings on top, however, so if you see these signs in the firebox, check to be sure the water didn't originate on top—the fittings are easily replaced, while a leaking tank implies buying a new water heater. An old water heater will have an accumulation of scale and rust at the bottom of the firebox. If you find soot around the firebox door, it means either faulty adjustment of the flame or a venting problem.

2) Examine the vent for soot or burned metal on the outside. Check the draft by turning up the water temperature knob until the heater comes on. Hold a lighted match next to the draft diverter at the base of the flue at the top of the unit; the flame should draw into the vent. If it doesn't, look at the flue pipe connecting the water heater with the vertical chimney. If this pipe dips or makes a long horizontal run before entering the chimney, it can be dangerous, allowing combustion products, including carbon monoxide, to escape into the house. You will want to ask the seller to correct this condition before you buy.

3) Observe the burner flame when the water heater is operating. A proper adjustment is blue; a yellow flame is improper. Turn down the water temperature and, when the flame goes out, probe into the baffle above the burner with your screwdriver or a wire. The presence of soot

42

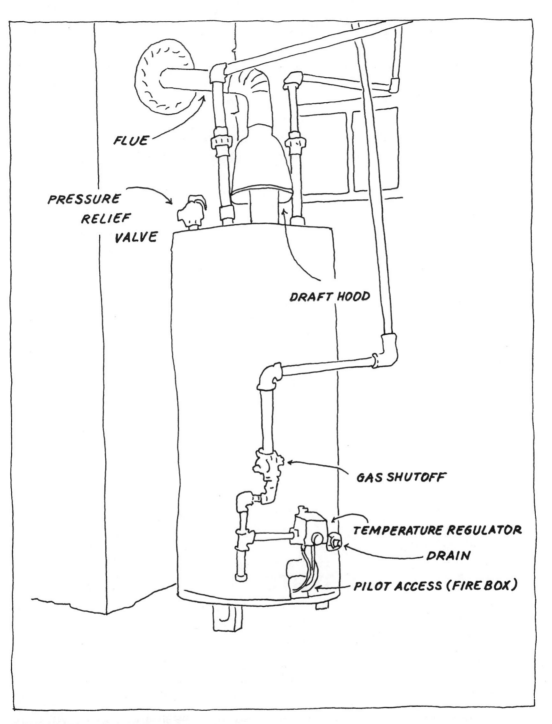

FLUE

PRESSURE
RELIEF
VALVE

DRAFT HOOD

GAS SHUTOFF

TEMPERATURE REGULATOR

DRAIN

PILOT ACCESS (FIRE BOX)

Natural gas hot-water heater

here indicates poor combustion. A plumber will be required to make the necessary adjustment.

4) If you hear a rumbling, popping noise when the water is heating, it is a sign of sediment accumulation, possibly several inches thick, on the bottom of the tank. The noise is caused by water trapped in the sediment heating into steam (you may have solid limestone stuck onto the bottom of the tank in a hard-water area). This accumulation of sediment reveals that the tank has not been drained periodically, and that the water heater is operating inefficiently and may soon require replacement.

5) On top of the tank you will find a cold water inlet and a hot water outlet. Identify these by touching them (the cold water line may be warm for a foot or so back from the heater). Do they correspond to the letters "h" and "c" stamped on the top of the tank? Sometimes plumbers accidentally reverse them, with a resulting loss of efficiency in the unit. You should also find a pressure relief valve (PRV) either on a third pipe out of the top, or on the hot water line. A hot water heater without such a relief valve could blow up, should its internal thermostat fail.

6) If you find water on the floor under the hot water heater, trace its source. The PRV could have released it, in which case it should be replaced or the water heater repaired. There may be a drip from the drain cock at the bottom, which probably can be fixed with a new washer. If the water came from within the unit, you may assume that it is about to fail completely.

ELECTRICAL SYSTEM Inspecting your electrical system involves finding out what kind of service you have and looking for unsafe wiring. A good place to begin is at the electric meter, which is usually located on an outside rear wall of the building. Less commonly it is found inside, on a back porch. If you have an overhead service "drop" from a power pole, you can see whether two or three wires are connected to the service mast (the 2-inch steel pipe above the meter). Two wires (one "hot" and one "neutral") mean that you have 120v current at the meter. Three wires (two hot wires of opposite polarity and a neutral wire) give you both 120v and 240v current. The meter itself may have useful information printed on its face, below the dials showing power consumption. If the meter reads 15a or 30a and 120v, you know that you have an old installation, with minimum current flow and no 240v current. (It's possible that your meter will indicate 110v or 115v current; these strengths are sometimes found and are not very different from the more widespread 120v current.)

The meter on a recent installation will read 60a or greater, and 240v current. This is an advantage, since it allows you to use appliances such as an electric range or electric clothes dryer. You are also likely to have more circuits and a generous supply of electrical outlets in the house. In an older house, a meter with a higher amperage rating and 240v current suggests that some rewiring and modernization have been undertaken. (Note: some meters have no information printed on them; in this case you will have to infer the capacity of the system from the circuit panel or fuse box.)

Look for the fuse box or circuit breaker panel. A breaker panel is often located right next to the meter, in which case it will be in a weatherproof housing. Pull the hinged cover out from the bottom, lift it up and slide it into the groove perpendicular to the top of the housing, where it will catch, leaving you both hands free to make notes on the number and kind of circuits you find. The "breakers" are switches that automatically click off in the event of an overload and can be reset by hand. You can use them to shut off any single circuit. Each breaker switch should have a rated amperage printed on it. Paired switches control 240v circuits. A breaker panel will have a main switch. It is usually the large, 240v paired switch at the top of the panel, although sometimes it has its own separate housing. A good installer or careful owner may have labeled each switch with the area of the house or the appliance it serves, saving you some guesswork.

Older houses, and even some newer installations, will have fuse boxes. A good place to look for them is on the back porch, at the top of the basement stairs, or high on a wall in the kitchen (where one may be concealed inside a cupboard). Open the little steel door carefully, as fuse boxes contain exposed wiring. Some safer designs involve flipping a main switch to "off" position before the door will open. Fuse boxes have varied widely in design. Inside you should find a main switch, perhaps of the "knife" variety, and a number of Edison, or plug, fuses, which screw in like a light bulb. Note the ampere rating on each.

Although it is possible to use plug fuses of up to 30 amps rating, don't use one rated higher than 15 amps unless advised by an electrician that it is all right in your house. Consider a circuit "overfused" where you find a plug fuse greater than 15 amps. It is difficult to know the condition of the wiring in an older home, and especially what alteration may have been made in the way of reducing its load capacity.

Cylindrical fuses, known as "cartridge fuses," are rated for higher amperages and will be found where 240v current is carried.

How many circuits do you have? You may have one fuse for every circuit, or you may have a pair of fuses on the main switch and another pair for each of two circuits, adding up to a total of six for two 15-amp circuits.

Wherever a system has been improved or added onto, you may find a fuse box and a circuit breaker panel, with a combination of old and new wiring, resulting in a very complicated arrangement of switches, fuses, and circuit breakers. Ask the owner to explain it to you. If he can't, consult an electrician or the power service company representative.

As you tour the house, be alert for open junction boxes, missing cover plates on switches or outlets, and loose or uninsulated wires that could be a safety hazard or start a fire. Your 120v-240v tester won't light up when in contact with a 12v or 24v doorbell, thermostat, or telephone wiring, but should you find exposed 120v or 240v wiring, insist that the seller correct this hazard before you buy.

RECOGNIZING ELECTRICAL CONDUIT

Electric current is carried in many different types of conduit or wiring:

1) Conduit *per se,* properly called "electrical metallic tubing," or more simply EMT, is galvanized steel pipe which might be confused with water pipe. This conduit comes only in ten-foot lengths, each piece bearing the seal of the Underwriters Laboratories. The heavier grades are joined with threaded couplings, while the lighter variety, or "thin-walled conduit," is connected with bushings quite different from anything you'd see on water pipe. Thin-walled conduit is frequently bent to go around corners, which is seldom done with steel water pipe (copper water pipe is usually bent, but its color is so distinctive it would

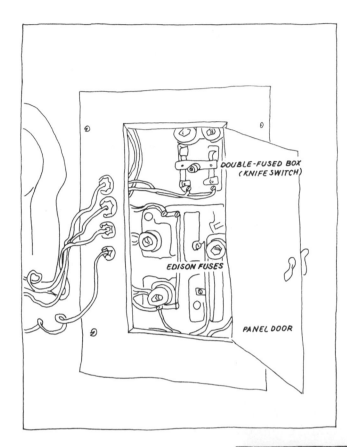

DOUBLE-FUSED BOX
(KNIFE SWITCH)

EDISON FUSES

PANEL DOOR

Three-circuit fuse box

Electric meter

be hard to confuse it with electrical conduit). Electrical conduit, of course, will connect to junction boxes, outlets, and switches, which obviously won't hold water!

2) A second kind of electrical conduit, used extensively, is flexible armored cable, made of galvanized steel wound in a tight spiral.

3) Plastic-covered "nonmetallic sheathed cable" has a characteristic flat shape, with its performance specifications printed on the outside. It's often called "Romex cable," after a common brand name.

4) "Knob-and-tube" installations consist of two parallel strands of insulated black wire strung several inches apart on porcelain knobs, protected by porcelain tubes where they go through timbers and beams. This is an obsolete method of installing wiring in houses; it may be safe where it is sealed inside a plaster wall, but should be considered hazardous where exposed to traffic, as in attics and basements.

5) Remodeling jobs often add convenience outlets and switches by using a type of flat steel conduit, known as "surface raceway" (or by brand names such as "Wiremold" or "Walkerduct"), which snaps together on the surface of a wall. It is perfectly safe.

6) All of the above forms of wiring are acceptable, but there is one more, commonly found in older houses, that is not safe. This is the thin, plastic-covered, two-strand wire sold in every hardware store and commonly called lamp cord. Lamp cord is suitable only to replace a cord on a clock or a radio, or to use as a short extension cord for a single appliance that doesn't draw much current. It is dangerous when tacked onto a wall to provide extra outlets, to which the unwary householder may be tempted to attach a miscellany of appliances. When overloaded beyond its capacity, the flimsy lamp cord can heat up and cause a fire.

OPERATING SYSTEMS CHECK SHEET

HEATING SYSTEM: natural gas _____oil _____electric _____coal _____
hot water _____steam _____warm air, gravity _____forced _____
operating _____safety pilot _____humidifier, operating _____
filter, clean _____dirty _____none _____flue, good _____poor _____
Observations: _____

AIR CONDITIONER _____operating _____

FURNACE ROOM VENTILATION: good _____fair _____poor _____
door: fireproof _____wood _____none _____

PLUMBING: galvanized _____copper _____plastic _____lead _____
leak: supply line _____drain _____location _____
Observations: _____

WATER SOFTENER _____

HOT WATER HEATER: size _____condition, new _____old _____
operating _____hot and cold reversed? _____PRV _____
corrosion on fittings? _____flue, condition: good _____bad _____

ELECTRICAL SYSTEM: number of wires to meter _____circuit breakers _____
fuses _____overfused? _____main switch, yes _____no _____
number of circuits: 120v _____240v _____total amps _____
OBSERVATIONS:_____

_____

SEE BACK OF BOOK FOR DETACHABLE CHECK SHEETS

POSTSCRIPT:
INSPECTING THE SOLAR HOME

If you are considering a house with solar energy, ask to see last winter's utilities bills and compare energy consumption with the normal requirements of a comparable house. Remember, you must have a conventional heating plant as a back-up system, adequate to heat the house completely by itself. Evaluate its capacity relative to the size of the house, and inspect it thoroughly along the guidelines given for furnaces.

Any solar house should be more tightly sealed and better insulated than a "normal" house because (in terms of your investment) the heat you are conserving is very expensive.

PASSIVE SYSTEMS A passive system is easy to check out; the storage wall must be one foot or more thick, oriented south, with a black surface facing the sun. It must be insulated with double-thickness glass on the outside. Check the automatic back-draft damper or check valve to see that it is working; it is usually made of very light plastic that will move in the slightest air current, to prevent cold air from entering the house from the heating area on sunless days.

If your passive system has glass walls insulated with styrofoam beads, operate the blowers to be sure all of them evacuate evenly. The beads in these walls are difficult to balance.

Solar greenhouses require lots of thermal storage, perhaps in the form of water-filled drums. The greenhouse should be double-glazed, well caulked and sealed.

ROOF COLLECTORS
Any system with roof collectors should provide protection against snow sliding off after a storm, either in the form of a catchment area or devices to slow up the slide.

Beware of collector areas that are too small. You will need a collector area one-third to one-half of your house area; a very well insulated house may be on the low side of this ratio. Don't buy a system of collectors that has moving parts, such as those that track or focus the sun. These require continual maintenance, which a homeowner might find difficult and therefore neglect.

Fluid system collectors should be steel or copper. Beware of plastic unless it has proven resistance to sunlight. Aluminum will corrode rapidly when in contact with any other metal, such as the copper piping. Collectors should provide for expansion, since they will experience a temperature range of more than 220° F. Any large array of collectors should have an expansion tank or a pressure relief valve to allow the system to bleed off in case the power to the pump should fail on a sunny day. The collector loop should have a check valve to prevent the fluid from flowing backwards at night or on cloudy days and cooling the house. Fluid collectors must be installed in a "reverse-return" pattern, where the total length of inlet plus outlet pipe is the same in each collector. This pattern equalizes the flow rate through them. If you have access to an electronic sensor or other thermometer that can measure the temperature rise across the collector system on a sunny day, look for at least a 15° F temperature rise from the inlet to the outlet pipe. A flow rate meter in the system should indicate a flow of at least .02 gallons per minute per square foot of collector surface. You must assure yourself that the system isn't plugged up somewhere.

In either a fluid or air system, check the operation of the solar controller, which determines whether the solar collector system or the back-up heating plant should run. It is triggered by two sensors (also called thermistors): one in the collectors and one in the storage tank. If the collectors are functioning but there is no reserve heat in the storage tank, the conventional heating plant (back-up system) should run. The solar and the conventional systems may run simultaneously or separately. The solar controller will have a light to indicate when the collectors are working. With a fluid system, operate the pumps to make sure they work.

51

AIR SYSTEMS

An air system should have a filter on the return air run, just behind the blower; inspect it to see if it is dirty and needs to be replaced.

A critical part in a solar air system is the damper, which shuts on cold days to prevent cold air from reaching the heat exchanger that preheats water for the hot water heater. A leak here could allow cold air on a subzero day to freeze the pipes in the heat exchanger. Such a leaking damper is difficult to detect ordinarily, because a small air leak here doesn't much decrease the warmth of the air in the heated air flow to the house, while it allows cold air to reach that crucial heat exchanger. Air systems are difficult to inspect because small leaks in the conduits are hard to notice, while they will decrease the overall efficiency of the system. You can check the flow rate if a meter is built in: it should be two cubic feet per minute of air per square foot of collector area.

FLUID SYSTEMS

The majority of solar installations use fluid collecting systems. Some are filled with an organic silicone-based oil. It doesn't require anti-freeze; it is chemically inert (causes no corrosion) and lasts indefinitely, as long as it doesn't leak out. Unfortunately, the extremely low surface tension of the oil allows it to leak profusely through even microscopic holes where water wouldn't go through, and it is very expensive to replace. With an oil-filled system, inspect every joint, pump, valve, and fitting carefully for oil stains that would indicate a leak. Check the mechanical room carefully, too. The oil system has an automatic filler.

Water-filled systems are either protected by anti-freeze or are of the "drain-down" type. In the drain-down system, a valve automatically opens to drain the collectors when the temperature falls below 35° F, so that they won't freeze. The idea is good, but many systems installed by amateurs or careless plumbers are not designed so that every single piece of pipe slopes down perfectly to drain completely. And if the system is set up to work only when electrical power is available to activate the solenoid switch of the drain valve, a power failure occurring at the same time as unseasonably low temperatures (such as during an ice storm) can cause the whole collector system to freeze.

For the above reasons, fluid collectors commonly use ethylene glycol anti-freeze to protect the water in the collector loop. The disadvantage of ethylene glycol is that it oxidizes slowly to form glycolic acid. It must be checked at least once a year, and drained completely every so often to prevent overacidity that will corrode the pumps, pipes, and valves. Use litmus paper (obtainable from a scientific equipment supply store) to check for acidity. The anti-freeze and water solution should be slightly basic.

Inspect the plumbing of any fluid system using water to ensure that no dissimilar metals have been used. If copper is used, all fittings must be copper or brass, never steel or aluminum. Even an insulated coupling will not completely eliminate corrosion where dissimilar metals are used, because an electrical path forms in the fluid itself. Ask for assurance that any plastic pipe used is designed for high temperature and pressure (such as high-temperature polyvinyl chloride). Most common plastic will fail under the stress of varying temperatures in a solar collector system.

INSULATION
Every inch of pipe in the system, including the collector loop and the hot water heater preheat, must be insulated. You should expect 1 inch to 1½ inches of insulation on pipes, including those inside walls, not only to conserve heat during cold weather but to prevent overheating the house in warm weather when you are still using the solar collectors to provide domestic hot water. The pumps and valves won't be insulated.

Storage tanks should be insulated to a value of R-25, or at least six inches, depending on the type of insulation chosen. Where they are buried in the ground, the insulation must be waterproof. Any water leaking into the insulation around a storage tank will allow heat to escape into the ground. A metal storage tank below ground should be fitted with an electrode of some active metal, preferably magnesium, which is itself buried, protecting the tank in the same way as ships are protected from corrosion when "in mothballs."

SOLAR SYSTEM CHECK SHEET

PASSIVE SYSTEM: storage wall _____ floor _____ double-glazed _____

bead wall, working _____ not working _____ none _____

check valve, working _____ not working _____ none _____

ROOF COLLECTORS: adequate _____ not adequate _____

material, plastic _____ steel _____ copper _____

aluminum _____ check valve _____ reverse-return _____

MECHANICAL: solar controller, operating _____ air, damper operating _____

blower, operating _____ pump, operating _____

conduits, insulated _____ storage, insulated _____

FLUID SYSTEM: oil _____ water, drain-down _____ anti-freeze _____

Ph, acceptable _____ not acceptable _____ leak _____

OBSERVATIONS: _____

_____

SEE BACK OF BOOK FOR DETACHABLE CHECK SHEETS

CHAPTER FIVE: INSPECTING LIVING AREAS

This chapter discusses the inspection of bedrooms, living rooms, dining rooms, and dens or family rooms. The procedure described will later be used in bathrooms and kitchen. Additional instructions are given in Chapters Six and Seven for inspecting plumbing fixtures, ventilation, and appliances. Inspect the walls, ceiling, windows, doors, floors, etc., of each room before starting on the next room. Begin by switching on all lights and opening curtains if they are closed.

CEILING Examine the ceiling, giving special attention to the edge where the ceiling meets the exterior wall. Look at the surface as a whole. Are there sagging or peeling sections of wallpaper (not merely an unglued edge); rough, crumbling, or uneven areas of plaster? Does the finish of the plaster change abruptly in one or more areas, indicating

55

it has been repaired? Are there areas of discoloration or water stains (especially in fiberboard or acoustical tile ceilings)? If the ceiling is in perfect condition, skip the next three paragraphs.

Rough, uneven, or patched areas that have been repainted suggest a leak which has been fixed. Estimate or ask how long ago the ceiling was repaired or painted. Find out what lies above this particular ceiling: is it the roof, an attic, or another room, possibly a bathroom? In an older home it's common to find a major repair of a ceiling beneath a bathroom — in thirty or forty years someone has almost certainly let the tub run over!

A damp area, or water damage that has not been repaired, or even a very recent paint job over some damage, requires investigation. If the damage is in the center of the ceiling or near an inside wall and there's a bathroom above, you will suspect leaking plumbing fixtures or drains. If no bath is overhead, it could be a leaking roof. Make a note to inspect the attic (if there is one) and the roof over this area.

If the damaged part of the ceiling lies close to an exterior wall, perhaps continuing down that wall, the cause is likely to be a leaking roof or a defective gutter (which might only be full of debris). Inspect the corresponding areas of roof and gutter.

WALLS Now look at the walls, especially around and underneath windows. Watch for peeling wallpaper and blistered plaster indicating water damage, or cracks that reveal structural shifting. Look for separation of one wall from another, or of a wall from the ceiling. See whether there are cracks between the wall and window frame, or around the door molding (especially where there is an outside door) and behind any wooden trim. If you don't find any cracks or blemishes, go on to the inspection of the windows.

Where you do find peeling wallpaper or blistered paint or plaster on a wall of a room (other than the bathroom) occurring from the top of the wall downward, you may attribute it to (exterior wall) a roof or gutter problem — (interior wall) leaking roof or plumbing. Make a note on the check sheet and carry out your inspection of the rooms or attic above and of the roof with special caution.

If you find water damage only under a window, the window frame

56

itself may need sealing, or the roof overhang above it may need repair. Examine the outside of the window and the roof overhang. On the other hand, a low window on the ground floor may have been wet by a carelessly placed sprinkler.

Water damage observed only at the base of a wall on the first story may be seen when the wall is partially below ground level, as in a semibasement or "garden level" room. A brick wall can sometimes draw up water like a wick from damp soil. In this case you might find blistered plaster and fine crystals of mineral leached out of the mortar and deposited on the inside by evaporation. Here, correction of the drainage around the house may improve the situation.

Caution: whenever you find linoleum, vinyl, or wood paneling on exterior walls at basement level or up to a few feet above ground on the first floor, you may suspect an attempt to cover up a wall damaged by moisture. Pry behind a corner of the paneling to inspect the surface of the wall beneath; look around the edges of windows where the paneling is fitted, and along the floor, for telltale signs of fine white crystals or sandy, crumbled mortar. Inspect the edges of the panel and the floor next to the wall for water stains.

CRACKS Most older plaster walls have slight cracks, caused by shrinking when the plaster dried or minor settling of the house framing. These may be fairly long, but in an older house, if they are thin enough to be covered with a coat of good paint, they are no cause for alarm.

Cracks to beware of in any type of wall are: 1) cracks that extend right through the wall and are visible on the other side, especially on an exterior wall; 2) cracks that have been filled or repaired in the past and which have reopened, revealing that the motion that caused the crack is still active; 3) any crack between walls, or between an exterior wall and the ceiling, suggesting separation of the exterior wall from the house. A crack or wall separation larger than ¼ inch in an older house, or a smaller crack in a recently built home, is occasion for a professional opinion. Make a note on your check sheet in red.

Cracks around window frames are common in old houses and may not be structurally serious. They should be sealed both inside and out, once the house is purchased, to prevent drafts and loss of heat in winter.

WINDOWS Open and close each window. Note whether any panes are broken, whether the windows are weatherstripped, and see if the hardware is in good condition. Do they lock? If you find double-glazed windows or storm windows, give them a plus. Are screens fitted to every window that is made to open? If not, ask the owner whether he has screens in storage for all windows. Windows that refuse to open usually have only been painted shut. They can be reopened with patience, hard work, and such tools as a pry bar, a utility knife, or a serrated tool made expressly for the purpose and sold in paint stores.

Examine the wood or metal frames and the sash around the window for rotten wood or rusted steel. Aluminum window frames are freer from corrosion (except where a high concentration of salt is in the air). They do conduct heat away from the house more readily, and are more likely to become bent than wood or steel.

If counterweighted or "double-hung" windows slide up and down but don't stay in position, check for broken or missing cords. You may find pulleys at the top of the slides. Iron weights will be concealed inside the window frames. They can be reconnected to the windows with new sash cords, but it is a job requiring some craftsmanship, as the window molding must be pried off the wall and put back again.

DOORS The fit of doors in their frames is a valuable clue to the structural condition of a house. You can safely assume that all door frames and doors were perfectly rectangular when the house was new. Open and close each door, including closet doors. Does it fit the door frame closely at the sides and top? Are both door and frame rectangular? If this is true for all the doors in a house, you can be confident that the structure has not sagged and the foundations have not settled unevenly. If the door sticks, or won't close completely, examine the frame. Is it rectangular, or do the sides slant to form a parallelogram? If this is the case, the house has shifted or the framing is warped. Door frames that sag or lean toward the center of the house usually indicate warped, inadequate floor joists or a sinking foundation at the center. (Check to see whether the floor joists and beams, as viewed from underneath, are adequate.)

Door frames leaning toward the exterior walls suggest that the foundation on that side is settling or leaning away from the house. If you noticed that the basement floor was humped, heaved, or badly cracked, part of the foundation may have risen because of earth swelling. The vertical motion of floor supports may have distorted the door frames. Whenever you find door frames noticeably out of rectangular, as in any of the situations described above, seek an expert opinion.

If the door frames are rectangular, but the door sticks or won't close easily, the problem may be: 1) too much paint on the door or frame; 2) warping of the door or frame; 3) woodwork swollen by moisture; 4) loose or damaged hardware, including hinges, latch, or striker plate. Consider each of these possibilities. Check the hinges by grasping both doorknobs and pulling the door toward you. Note the condition on the check sheet. Doors—unless they are of unusual size or are antiques—are comparatively easy to replace. If you're a do-it-yourselfer, consult one of the home repair manuals for advice in repairing or replacing them.

While checking the doors, be sure that the hardware works properly. Do locks function as they should? Exterior doors should be fitted with deadbolt locks for safety.

FLOORS
Floors that bounce or sag may result from undersized floor joists, joists inadequately braced, or from damage to the timbers. To find the cause, return to the basement or crawl space underneath the floor in question. Are the joists visibly in good condition? Are any spans more than ten feet in length supported by beams? Are the joists undersized (less than 2" x 8") or spaced too far apart—more than 16 inches on centers (or 24 inches in the case of larger joists, such as 2" x 10"). If the joists are undersized or too far apart, it may be advisable to add support from below, such as a new post and beam. Adequately sized joists that spring or bounce can be stabilized with cross-bracing. A carpenter's manual will describe the procedure.

Sometimes a floor will make a slapping noise when you walk on it. This is usually a sign that a plywood subfloor is not tightly nailed or glued to the joist beneath it. You can stop the slapping by inserting shims and glue on top of the joists (where they are accessible).

Squeaks can be cured by lubricating the wood strip in question with talcum powder or light oil. Where this fails, renailing is possible. See one of the home repair manuals listed in the bibliography (especially *Sunset Magazine's Basic Home Repairs,* p. 67).

A variety of hard and soft woods are used for flooring. In many older houses oak strips were laid in the living and dining rooms, and pine or fir (which are softwoods) upstairs in the bedrooms. Many people mistake a nicely finished softwood floor for hardwood, but while a softwood floor can be attractive, it is easily scratched and doesn't keep a finish as well. In general, the resinous softwoods such as pine, fir, or larch can be identified by the presence of small knots and a yellowish color.

Resilient floor covering such as vinyl or linoleum may conceal a hardwood floor beneath, but don't count on it. To discover what's underneath, look for a loose corner or lift the metal grille of a cold-air return. If you intend to restore a wood floor presently beneath linoleum or vinyl sheet or tile, it will be a laborious process to tear off the floor covering, sand off the glue, and refinish the surface of the wood. If you're satisfied with the resilient floor covering, make a note of its condition. Sheet vinyl is soft and cuts or tears easily. Asphalt tile is hard but brittle. The old sheet linoleum that was made thirty or more years ago sometimes will outlast modern materials, but the old patterns may not be to your taste.

Wall-to-wall carpet has many advantages. It reduces sound transmission and it is easier to maintain than a wood floor. Builders like it because it covers up a cheap plywood floor. (This is likely to be the case if the house you're considering was built after 1955.) The carpet may have a loose edge or corner which you can lift up to see what kind of floor is underneath. If you're satisfied to have carpet, examine it for quality. Is it worn or stained? If it looks brand new, get down and examine the fibers. Many shag carpets look nice when first laid but deteriorate remarkably quickly. Pry the tufts apart with your fingers: if you can see the backing readily, you may be looking at an inferior grade. Brush the pile lightly with your hand. Good carpet should spring back, not lie flat. Check the edges to see that they have been cut and fitted neatly, and be sure that there aren't loose edges at doorways and halls to trip you. When opening and closing doors, make certain that they clear the carpet easily.

ELECTRICAL OUTLETS You switched on a light as you entered the room. Now switch on any other lights to ensure that they work properly. Count the number of electrical outlets. The Electrical Code requires that no point along the edge of the floor should be more than six feet from an outlet. This requirement is for new construction. Older houses may have fewer, even no, outlets in a room, so look carefully. Reject as unsafe any outlets that are screwed or nailed onto the surface of the wall or baseboard, and are connected to a recessed outlet by lamp cord. If you don't have three or four standard outlets in a room, you will be tempted to use extension cords, which are potential fire hazards and may trip someone. Consider adding outlets. Make a note to consider this option at the end of your inspection.

What kind of outlets do you have? Do they have two, or three slots? If two, then you may not have a grounded electrical system. Test with your circuit tester by grounding one of the probes onto the screw at the center of the coverplate and inserting the other probe into each of the two parallel slots, one at a time (hold the probe only by the insulation). You will see the test lamp glow as you connect the hot side with the grounding screw. A properly grounded screw in the coverplate allows you to connect appliances that require grounding by using a three-hole adapter and the "pig-tail" which connects under the grounding screw in the coverplate.

Where all the outlets have three slots, you can be reasonably sure to have a grounded system. Test an outlet: your lamp should glow when the probes are inserted into the two parallel slots (hot and neutral) and when they are inserted into the hot side and the third opening, which is the ground. If the lamp glows when the probe is connected from ground to *each* parallel slot, you have detected a wiring fault or a 240v circuit. Make a note to consult the electrical service company or an electrician.

HEATING Find the source of heat for the room. If it is a branch of the central furnace, feel it with your hand. It should still be warm from your test of the furnace a few minutes ago (radiators take a much longer time to heat up—give them an hour or so). How is the heat source situated with regard to outside walls and windows? Where you

61

have a warm air system, is there a cold air return in the room or, if not, is the door undercut sufficiently to allow air circulation?

From the standpoint of comfort, the preferred location for hot air grilles, radiators, or baseboard registers is at the base of exterior walls. The cold air returns (in a warm air system) should be opposite them, on internal walls. Any other arrangement will result in uneven heating. Gravity systems, especially gravity-air systems, usually don't have the capacity to move heat to the perimeter of a house. Warm air registers often are on interior walls — this is one of the drawbacks of a gravity system.

If the room has its own heat source, such as a wall furnace or baseboard heat, turn it on. A gas wall furnace functions in much the same way as a larger furnace. The safest are vented horizontally through the wall and draw their combustion air from outside. As a badly placed vent may scorch the outside wall or passersby, inspect it to ensure that the wall is protected and that children and animals cannot burn themselves on it.

A wall furnace may also be vented vertically and draw its combustion air from the room itself. There's a risk of asphyxiation in a small, tightly closed room with one of these furnaces or a stove.

FIREPLACES
Kneel down and look up the chimney. Can you see light at the top? If so, it's a good sign that the chimney is open. If you can't, there may only be a built-in bend in the flue. Shine your flashlight up the chimney. Is the flue lined with tile, or do you see bricks and mortar? The latter (an unlined flue) can collect creosote and soot, constituting a fire danger. You may wish to have any flue, especially an unlined one, cleaned by a professional chimney sweep if it shows signs of heavy use.

Remove your head from the fireplace and test the damper to see whether it shuts and opens.

Are there any loose bricks in the fireplace or chimney? Are there cracks between bricks? Is the hearth solid? Is the back of the fireplace smoke-stained? If so, that's evidence the fireplace is usable. If it's not smoke-stained, ask the owner why not? Occasionally a good fireplace has never been used, but a virgin condition frequently indicates that the fireplace is only decorative. It may not even have a chimney! Smoke stains on the face of the mantel directly above the fireplace opening, on the other hand, can indicate a poor draft, a badly designed flue, or debris in the chimney.

The requirements of a good fireplace are: 1) sides and back made of firebrick, which is a tan, sandy color; 2) a depth of about 18 inches for openings up to 32 inches wide and a depth of 20 inches to 24 inches for wider openings; 3) sides that splay, or open outward toward the room, and the back inclined forward as it slopes upward, all in the shape of a reflector, to throw heat into the room; 4) an opening height less than the width; 5) a damper to close off any draft from the room when shut; 6) a flue opening not less than 1/10 the area of the fireplace opening; 7) a generous hearth.

The ideal fireplace to have in these days of energy shortages is the kind that recirculates and heats air from the room. It has cold air inlets at floor level off to the side of the fireplace and hot air risers several feet above them. The hollow andirons that purport to do the same thing are poor substitutes.

Test for proper draft by crumpling a couple of sheets of newspaper and lighting them at the top, so that the fire starts gradually. Avoid a sudden burst of flame in a cold fireplace: this will always blow smoke into a room.

LIVING AREA CHECK SHEET

ROOM: _____

CEILING: plaster _____sheetrock _____other _____

crack _____rough _____leak _____location _____

WALLS: plaster _____sheetrock _____other _____

crack _____rough _____leak _____location _____

WINDOWS: number _____cracked panes _____weatherstripped _____

double _____operating, yes _____no _____

hardware, satisfactory _____poor _____

DOORS: exterior _____fit _____hardware, satisfactory _____poor _____

interior _____fit _____hardware, satisfactory _____poor _____

FLOOR: wood _____lino/vinyl _____carpet _____condition _____

ELECTRICAL: light, operating _____outlets, number _____

HEATING: radiators _____grilles _____baseboard _____

wall furnace _____radiant _____thermostat _____

AIR CONDITIONER: _____

FIREPLACE: flue, lined_____unlined_____condition_____

damper, operating _____not operating _____none _____

OBSERVATIONS:_____

_____

SEE BACK OF BOOK FOR DETACHABLE CHECK SHEETS

CHAPTER SIX: THE KITCHEN

Turn on all lights and check the ceiling, walls, windows, and doors as described in the previous chapter. Is the floor suitable for kitchen use? Occasionally decorators are inspired to lay carpet in the kitchen, but this is a poor place for it, with spills of water and greasy liquids possible.

Examine the layout of the kitchen as a whole. Is there an eating area? The kitchen is the most popular room in the house and it is a favorite place for informal entertaining (as was the parlor for the Victorians). A breakfast nook or other informal eating area rates a plus. Imagine yourself working in the kitchen. Is there counter space on both sides of the sink? Does the arrangement of sink, stove, refrigerator, counter space, and cabinets make sense? Is it easy to get around and convenient to work in? Does an open refrigerator door block access to a doorway or to anything else of importance? Are there enough cabinets, including base cabinets for heavy pots and pans?

65

Count the electrical outlets. Having outlets in the right places is vital in a kitchen. They should optimally be found in the following places: 1) one or more at countertop level near the sink; 2) at the tabletop level on the wall in the eating area; 3) behind the refrigerator; 4) behind the stove, if gas. There will be a 240v outlet if you have an electric stove.

Now for the plumbing. Run water into the sink for a minute or so, first cold, then hot. Is there adequate pressure? Sometimes poor water pressure is caused by nothing more serious than a faucet aerator clogged with sand or rust. Low pressure on the hot side, but not the cold, suggests corroded fittings on the supply line somewhere between the hot water heater and the faucet — the hot line corrodes several times faster than the cold. If you find low hot water pressure but not cold, make a note to think about this problem again after you've checked the pressure in the bathroom.

Do the faucets drip after being shut off gently? Does water leak out from underneath the fixture where it meets the sink, indicating a leak in the faucet? These annoyances are fairly simple to repair.

Find the switch for the garbage disposal (it is often located underneath the sink countertop or on the wall behind the sink) and turn it on. Run it for a few seconds before turning on the water: a disposal in good condition should run smoothly when empty. Direct water into the disposal and run it a few more seconds until you are sure the water flushes out properly. At no time when running water into the sink should it back up. A slow or clogged drain is something you should ask the seller to have fixed before you buy.

Can you fit your hand into the opening of the disposal? A few models have so small an opening that the average person can't clean out the bottle caps, pieces of glass, and scrub brushes that often fall into them.

Having run water into the sink, kneel down and open the cabinet beneath it. Shine your flashlight on the drain. Look for water on it and on the floor underneath. The U-shaped drain is called a "P-trap." Feel the underside of it. Is it wet from a leak? Is it rough, indicating that it is about to rust through? Has it been taped together, revealing a lazy-man's repair that will have to be fixed again before long?

Look for leaks or drips on the supply lines that carry water to the faucets above. Do they have shut-off valves? These are good, as they permit changing a washer without shutting off water to the entire house.

Turn on the burners of the stove or cook top, and of the oven. As soon as they heat up, turn them off again. Is there a vent hood with fan over the cooking surface to take away odors, smoke, and grease? It should be vented to the outside. The cheaply installed hoods that draw air over a filter and blow it back into your face aren't really adequate.

A self-cleaning oven of the pyrolitic, or high-temperature, type is convenient. One of these will have directions for use printed on the panel near the controls. If you want to be sure it works, follow the directions and turn it on, locking the oven. An indicator light should come on. Within half an hour, while you are inspecting the remainder of the house, it should have attained full heat, giving off an unmistakable odor of hot metal. Before leaving, don't forget to shut it off. You shouldn't be able to open the oven door until the inside is cool.

A dishwasher with dishes stacked in it is probably in working order. To check it out, run it through the cycles quickly, manually advancing the control as soon as it has rinsed, washed, rinsed again, drained, and dried — a few minutes in each mode.

Inspect the refrigerator and freezer to ensure that the gaskets around the doors are tight, and that frost-free operation is in order where indicated.

67

KITCHEN CHECK SHEET

CEILING: plaster _____ sheetrock _____ other _____

crack _____ rough _____ leak _____ location _____

WALLS: plaster _____ sheetrock _____ other _____

crack _____ rough _____ leak _____ location _____

WINDOWS: number _____ cracked panes _____ weatherstripped _____

double _____ operating, yes _____ no _____

hardware, satisfactory _____ poor _____

DOORS: exterior _____ fit _____ hardware, satisfactory _____ poor _____

interior _____ fit _____ hardware, satisfactory _____ poor _____

FLOOR: wood _____ lino/vinyl _____ carpet _____ condition _____

ELECTRICAL: light, operating _____ outlets, number _____

HEATING: radiators _____ grille _____ baseboard _____

wall _____ furnace _____ radiant _____ thermostat _____

DINING AREA: yes _____ no _____   COUNTER SPACE: yes _____ no _____

PLUMBING: sink, good _____ old _____ double _____ faucet leak _____

shut offs _____ P-trap leak _____ drainage, good _____ poor _____

water pressure _____ disposal, operating _____ none _____

DISHWASHER: operating _____ not operating _____ none _____

STOVE: gas _____ electric _____ operating _____ old _____ vent _____

REFRIGERATOR: operating _____ old _____ FREEZER _____ CABINETS _____

OBSERVATIONS: _____

_____

SEE BACK OF BOOK FOR DETACHABLE CHECK SHEETS

68

CHAPTER SEVEN: THE BATHROOM

Inspect the bathroom ceiling and walls as you did those of the other rooms. Is there paint peeling off the ceiling over the shower? The bathroom is the only place in the house where there is often enough moisture to peel paint off the walls or ceiling from condensation alone. Remedies include improving the ventilation and repainting with exterior grade or marine quality paint. Never discount entirely the possibility of a leak in the ceiling, however. If you find cracks in the plaster, peeling wallpaper, or damaged sheetrock, you should suspect a leak. If there's a room or attic above, make a note to check the floor and walls when you get there; if a roof, inspect it carefully for faults.

Open and close, and lock the window, if there is one. If there is no window, there should be an exhaust fan, or at least a good vent, to carry away moist air and odors. Is there a light near the mirror (which in turn should be located above the lavatory sink)? One more essential to complete the working facilities here is an electrical outlet within easy reach of the mirror. Many older homes, unfortunately, lack outlets in bathrooms.

WATER PRESSURE A good test is to turn on the hot water in the basin and shower. Now, keeping your eyes on the shower spray, flush the toilet. With adequate water pressure, the shower spray should be only slightly affected by the water running into the toilet tank. If the shower is markedly affected, imagine yourself under it when this happens. Poor water pressure may be caused by an inadequate supply to the house as a whole. More commonly, below-normal pressure to one or a few fixtures is a symptom of corroded fittings, usually on the hot water line. Those fittings most subject to corrosion are (in the case of galvanized steel pipe) the elbows and nipples in the wall behind the tub or shower, the fittings on the top of the hot water heater, and wherever two dissimilar metals in the plumbing join.

Flush the toilet a second time to ensure that the drain line is running freely. The water should spiral down and out as smoothly as it did the first time. A sluggish toilet drain (where there is a connection to a sewer) is possible in either of the following situations: If the bowl empties freely when flushed the first time, but more sluggishly upon subsequent flushings, the drain line is probably obstructed well below the toilet itself. This will be the case if any other nearby drain, or a drain immediately below, is involved. On the other hand, if the bowl empties slowly only when waste is present (and then perhaps with the help of a plunger), there's likely to be an obstruction within the toilet itself—a common occurrence when young children are present to drop hairbrushes, etc., into the bowl. In this case, other drains in the house run freely if they are not beset with their own localized problems.

Whenever you find any drainage problem, mark the check sheet accordingly and ask the seller to have the drains cleaned or repaired before you conclude the purchase.

Having flushed the toilet, look around the base for leaks. Water on the floor here usually indicates a faulty wax seal between the toilet and the soil line. This condition is generally simple to repair but, if it has persisted for a long time, the floor underneath may be rotten. Grasp the toilet bowl with both hands and rock it back and forth to test the strength of the floor and the anchor screws.

When the toilet tank has filled, listen for the water supply to shut off.

Run cold water in the lavatory sink. Now look underneath for leaks, running your hand across the underside of the P-trap to check for moisture or roughness that would indicate corrosion and an incipient leak. Are there shut-off valves on the supply lines? There should be no leakage of water from underneath the faucet itself.

CHECKING WATER QUALITY Follow this procedure if the house has its own water supply. Taste and smell water from the sink. Wash your hands in it with soap to test its hardness. Does it take an unusual amount of soap to form a lather? Lift the toilet tank lid and inspect the color and appearance of the water in the tank. Is it discolored in any way, or cloudy? Are there stains in the toilet tank or bowl, lavatory sink, or tub? The following table will help you troubleshoot a variety of common water-quality problems.

COMMON WATER-QUALITY PROBLEMS

Problem	Cause	Remedy
"Hard water"	Dissolved magnesium and calcium	Water softener
"Red water": red stains on porcelain fixtures; metallic taste; red slime in toilet tank; water turns reddish upon exposure to air	Iron compounds, iron bacteria, or manganese	Water softener or oxidizing filter
"Acid water": red stains in sinks served by steel pipe; blue-green stains on copper and brass fixtures; metal parts corroded	Usually dissolved carbon dioxide; rarely, a mineral acid	Neutralizing filter, or chemical feeder supplying alkaline solution
"Rotten egg" odor or taste; metallic fixtures corroded; fine black particles in water and silverware turns black	Hydrogen sulfide or sulfates	Oxidizing filter, chlorination, or sand filter
"Off" taste (but not rotten egg); salty, brackish, oily	High mineral content or presence of organic matter; water may be contaminated	Determine source of contamination; filter and chlorinate
Turbidity: dirty or muddy	Silt or organic matter	Sand filter
Bacteria (indicated by laboratory analysis)	Contamination from sewage	Correct sewage disposal; chlorinate, and use charcoal filter

NOTE: See USDA's *Treating Farmstead and Rural Home Water Systems*, Farmer's bulletin #2248, U. S. Government Printing Office #001-000-03558-4.

Before leaving the bathroom, inspect the tile on the shower wall for tightness and for a good water seal. Tap any suspect areas sharply with your fingers, especially around the fixtures and along the base of the shower wall. Looseness or softness here could indicate that substantial repairs are necessary to the wall behind.

Inspect the floor for water stains or other damage around the outside of the tub or shower (especially if you noted water stains on the ceiling of the room below).

Lastly, if you haven't already done so, find the furnace outlet or heater. If the latter, test it. Don't forget to close and open the bathroom door and check its hardware, as you did the doors to other rooms.

BATHROOM CHECK SHEET

CEILING: plaster _____ sheetrock _____ other _____ crack _____
rough _____ leak _____ location _____

WALLS: plaster _____ sheetrock _____ other _____ crack _____
rough _____ leak _____ location _____

WINDOW: operating, yes _____ no _____ hardware, condition _____

VENT _____ **FAN** _____ **LIGHT** _____ **CABINET** _____

ELECTRICAL OUTLETS, number _____

WATER PRESSURE: normal _____ below normal _____

TOILET: good _____ poor _____ leak at base _____

DRAINS: satisfactory _____ slow _____ clogged _____

BASIN: good _____ poor _____ faucet leak _____ no _____ P-trap leak _____
shut-offs _____ none _____

WATER QUALITY: discoloration _____ odor _____ satisfactory _____

TUB _____ **SHOWER** _____ grout required _____

HEATING: radiator _____ grille _____ baseboard _____ wall furnace _____

DOOR: fit, good _____ poor _____ hardware, good _____ poor _____

FLOOR: wood _____ tile _____ lino/vinyl _____ carpet _____ condition _____

OBSERVATIONS: _____

_____

SEE BACK OF BOOK FOR DETACHABLE CHECK SHEETS

CHAPTER EIGHT: THE ATTIC

The access to many attics is through a loose panel overhead in a hall or bedroom closet. Houses with additions may have more than one attic, so be sure to inspect them all. With an overhead panel, you will need your five-foot stepladder and your flashlight. Place the ladder securely under the access panel and remove the panel carefully by lifting it straight up with both hands and placing it to one side. Avoid tilting it or turning it over, as it may be covered with loose insulation, squirrel droppings, dust, spiderwebs, and other debris you don't want to fall into your eyes.

Climb to the top of the ladder and shine your flashlight around before entering. If there's a light, turn it on. If you have entered via a staircase or a conventional door, the attic may have partial or complete flooring. If it was via access panel, you most likely are looking at an attic with no floor, just the top of the joists (usually 2x4s or 2x6s) to which the

75

ceilings of the rooms below are attached. If you are planning to finish or enlarge the attic to provide space for another room, you must have at least 2x6 joists in the floor for sufficient strength.

In the case of an attic without any flooring, I advise you to venture no further unless: 1) your inspection of the ceiling and interior walls of the rooms below has disclosed blistered plaster, loose wallpaper, peeling paint, water stains, dampness, or any other suggestion that the roof may have leaked; *and* 2) you have good balance and are confident of your footing. If you can say "yes" to 1) and 2), raise yourself carefully through the access hole until your weight rests on the framing around it. Then walk through the attic to the areas where you suspect water entry, placing each foot carefully on the top of the joist or plank beneath you, keeping one hand always on a rafter or other steady support for balance. Go slowly. Never step between the joists onto insulation or lath, or you may very likely put your foot through the ceiling below.

Examine the underside of the roof for water stains or dampness. If there has been a recent rain or snow, you may find drips or damp places on the boards, shingles, or rafters overhead. If not, look carefully for discoloration. A pronounced leak may have left traces on the attic floor or insulation. Where you find any indication of a leak, you will want to inspect the roof above. Mark in red on your check sheet and look for this spot when you get onto the roof. If the seller tells you that the roof has been repaired, ask for receipts as proof.

VENTILATION All attics and crawl spaces must be ventilated—for comfort during summer in the rooms below; to relieve the load on air conditioning; to prevent excessive heat buildup from damaging the roof covering; and to eliminate moisture from the house, which can condense inside the attic in winter. Look for cross-ventilation as either: 1) screen openings under the edge of the roof, around the sides of the attic, combined with a vent or fan at the peak; 2) windows or vents at opposite ends of the attic.

If you are inspecting the attic during cold weather and find frost on the underside of the roof sheathing, or on nails protruding into the attic from the roof, this is a sure indication of inadequate ventilation. In other seasons, water stains or rusty nails are signs to look for. Vents must be kept open year-round.

A finished attic needs very good cross-ventilation, and perhaps air conditioning, to make it habitable in summer. I have seen attics converted into bedrooms, with no thought given to the ventilation required to prevent them from becoming ovens in summer.

INSULATION Except in mild parts of the country, attic insulation is essential. Not long ago it was considered a luxury, and you'll still find older homes without insulation in the attic, where the greatest home heating loss can occur. In an unfinished attic, the appropriate place for insulation is at the floor level. In cold climates, six inches is the recommended minimum, which means that insulation should cover 2x6 joists. There are many kinds of insulating material. It may be "poured" in bulk over the attic floor, or laid between joists in the form of batts (these are usually made of fiberglass). Any reflective foil or moisture barrier should be placed next to the warm room ceiling. If it has been incorrectly placed on top, moist air from the warm house will penetrate the fiberglass, spoil its insulating value, and possibly damage the ceiling.

In a finished attic used as living space, insulation should be within the walls and ceiling. Check carefully behind an electrical outlet, switch cover, or any other opening that will allow you to look between the inner and exterior walls.

WIRING An unfinished attic without a floor can give you a perspective on the kind of wiring used in the house. The electric wires for the ceiling light fixtures in the rooms below, and sometimes those for the wall outlets too, will run across the attic floor joists. You may find steel conduit, plastic-sheathed cable, or pairs of insulated wires running between porcelain insulators. The latter, called "knob-and-tube" wiring, not usually installed in homes since the 1920s, were designed to carry only 15 amps. The insulation on the wires becomes brittle with age and may fall off. Examine the wires closely (don't touch) for the quality of the covering. Never allow debris or items stored in the attic to touch this wiring, and don't cover it with insulation. Rewire before insulating.

77

FRAMING If you had previously noted any irregularity in the roof line when you looked at the outside of the house, now is the time to inspect the ridge board, rafters, etc., for any indication of warping or sagging. Look along the line of the rafters to check them for straightness. If they sag, it may be possible to brace them, but don't buy the house without an expert opinion from a carpenter or contractor as to the cost and feasibility of doing so.

ATTIC CHECK SHEET

FLOOR: size and spacing of joists _____flooring, yes _____

partial _____none _____

RAFTERS: size and spacing _____condition, acceptable _____

poor _____leak _____location _____none

VENTILATION: adequate _____inadequate _____none _____

INSULATION: floor _____walls _____roof _____none _____not visible _____

adequate _____not adequate _____

ELECTRICAL: wiring visible _____conduit _____knob and tube _____

OBSERVATIONS:_____

_____

SEE BACK OF BOOK FOR DETACHABLE CHECK SHEETS

CHAPTER NINE: THE WEATHER SIDE

You've finished inspecting the inside. The condition of interior walls and ceilings may have indicated some problem areas you will now want to look at closely: damp or water-stained walls relate to possible defective gutters and downspouts; wet basements to poor peripheral drainage; damaged ceilings to a faulty roof.

THE ROOF An important aspect of the design of the roof is its overhang. A generous overhang is both esthetic and practical. It protects the windows and walls from water, encourages better drainage away from the foundation, and shades windows from the summer sun. On the other hand, in cold climates an overhang can allow formation of an ice dam after a heavy snow, as the water runs off a roof warmed by an uninsulated attic (or the heat of the sun), only to freeze on the overhang. Additional runoff water, blocked by the ice, can find

Deteriorated asphalt shingles on roof, showing curling and loss of mineral covering

Wood shingles, soft and broken with age (leaking at this point)

its way through the shingles into the roof and walls. If you found evidence of water stains on a wall directly under the roof, and the roof (shingles, tile, or rolled roofing) appears sound, an ice dam may be the explanation. The cure may be to insulate and ventilate the attic, add wide flashings to the top of the overhang, or lay insulated thermal electric cable in the gutter.

Inspect the roof by climbing onto it or visually inspecting it from the ground or from surrounding buildings that offer vantage points. A useful trick is to use binoculars to view the roof. The most common roofing materials are rolled asphalt and asphalt shingles, wood shingles, tile, slate, and metal sheets—all of these on pitched roofs. Flat roofs usually are finished with built-up layers of composition felt and tar, often topped with gravel.

Always walk with care on any roof, but take extra caution with those of tile and slate. These are slippery and fragile materials that can crack or break from your weight. Tile, slate, and metal are long-lived, premium roofing materials. Ordinarily they will require only incidental repairs in the lifetime of a house. Wood, asphalt, and composition coverings have a useful life of ten to thirty years, depending upon exposure and thickness.

The south-facing part of any roof receives the most severe weathering. Examine it carefully, but keep in mind that it may have been replaced more recently than the remainder. With asphalt shingles, look for signs of excessive weathering, such as curling, cracks, or surfaces with the mineral facing washed away. Wooden shingles become cracked, broken, or soft and rotten when old. Tiles and slates may be broken or missing. Built-up composition becomes rough, pitted, or cracked with age; watch out for "bubbles," where air pockets have formed between the composition and the roof (you may detect them when you step on them). These should be repaired before they begin to leak.

Common sites of leaks are flashings around vents, chimneys, at valleys, and next to walls and cornices. The roof should be so designed that water does not stand in puddles at any point, especially around chimneys or skylights; inspect these carefully to see that they are well caulked and sealed. Probe possible problem areas with your fingers for softness, rotten wood, or rusted metal. Are the flashings well sealed with asphalt cement, especially on the uphill side?

83

Stone or brickwork on the roof is often neglected. All chimneys, cornices, etc., should be capped with cement, and mortar should be intact between bricks. Loose brick or stone at this height can be dangerous! Make sure that any masonry chimney is at least three feet above the roof that it passes through, and not less than three feet above the highest ridge within ten horizontal feet, to ensure a good draft within the fireplace. Take a look at all chimneys to make sure they are straight and solid.

Vents for plumbing, which release sewer gases, must extend at least 24 inches upward from the roof, and not be within ten feet of any door, window, or air intake.

Where you have identified leaks, you may want to ask the seller to have these repaired, or to take the cost of repairs into account in the selling price. If you buy the house, remember to repair any deteriorated areas of the roof before a leak develops that could spoil paint, wallpaper, or plaster on the ceilings and walls below. This inspection may be the last time you notice your roof until it gives you trouble.

GUTTERS It's a wise idea to have a look at gutters from above. In the vicinity of tall trees, gutters may require cleaning twice a year. Inspect them for debris, and for hanger straps in good condition. Once you have descended from the roof, examine all gutters from below. If it's raining, it's easy to spot leaking gutters. In dry weather, look for stains, peeling paint, water-etched brick, or rotten eaves and trim beneath them.

Downspouts that are cracked or full of leaves can cause as much havoc on both outside and interior wall finish as does a leaking roof. While you're looking at the downspouts, determine how water drains away from them. Poor drainage from downspouts is one of the commonest causes of a wet basement, and the easiest to fix. Where the ground doesn't slope adequately away from the house, good splashblocks or downspout extensions are in order. You may see downspouts directed into "dry wells" which connect with the city storm-drain system. These must be kept clean; if they're blocked up, the next rainstorm will let you know.

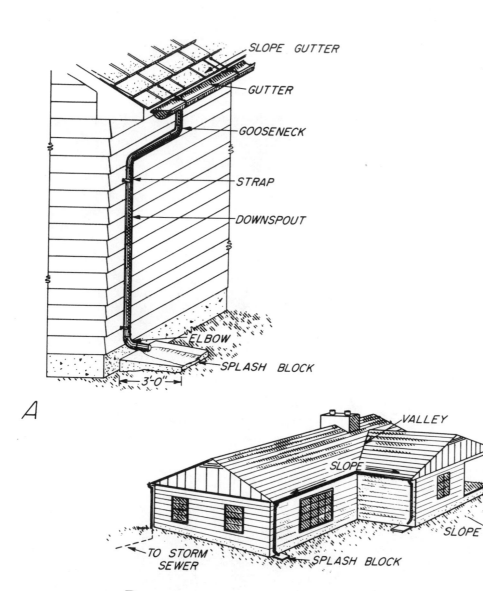

Installation of

(A) downspout, and

(B) gutter, showing slope and drainage away from foundation walls by splash block or by storm-sewer connection.

(Source: Forest Products Laboratory, Forest Service, USDA)

85

Damage caused by broken gutter: excessive weathering of wood, mortar lost from between bricks

Positive drainage away from the walls of a house is important. Inspect the soil next to any areas of the foundation where dampness in the basement was a problem. Do you find a low spot where water or snow might collect and percolate down a foundation wall? Are there bushes, flower plantings, or a lawn right next to a foundation wall, so that watering could cause the dampness problem? These are situations that you can remedy. Fill in low spots (perhaps underlaying plastic film), remove vegetation, and don't let watering wash the sides of the house.

While you're looking along ground level, note any wood in contact with the earth, or even within a few inches of it. Where you find such, probe with your screwdriver for softness that indicates termite damage or decay. In the South and East, homes may be provided with a metal termite shield on top of the foundation.

House exteriors are commonly of masonry, wood, or some form of composition or metal siding.

MASONRY
Masonry may be single course (one thickness of brick) or double. A double brick wall will have some courses partly or wholly laid with bricks end-to, so that the brick extends lengthwise into the wall. With any brick, concrete block, stone, or stucco exterior, the most important thing to watch for is a crack of any size (especially one that is visible on the inside as well). Remember, too, that missing mortar weakens a wall and allows leakage of air and heat.

WOOD SIDING
Problems here derive from moisture. Lack of sufficient roof overhang, or defective gutters, will let water run down the wall. Moisture can also enter the siding from inside, condensing within the wall during winter if there is no effective vapor barrier.

Stand close to the wall and sight along it for warped boards, cracks, or spaces between boards. Look for signs of decay at the ends of boards and around doors and window frames. If there are wood shingles on the walls, look for broken, warped, upturned, and rotten shingles. Wherever you see paint flaking or peeling off, examine the wood for softness, discoloration, and decay.

Within the last twenty years or so, many medium- to lower-priced houses have been finished with plywood siding, which is scored or grooved to simulate the appearance of vertical boards. It should not be in contact with the ground; inspect it for uneven weathering, splitting, or delamination.

Look around windows, and wherever two different materials join, watch for cracks that should be caulked. Take a look at trim, gables, exposed rafters or eaves, if you haven't already done so, and note whether they need repair or repainting.

PORCHES
Porches often are added after the initial construction of a house, sometimes on poorly prepared foundations. They may crack or lean away from the house, without necessarily being unsafe or implying that the house itself shares the problem. Climb any external stairs, perhaps bouncing a little on wooden stair treads. Are they firm and sound? If the porch seems to have major problems, record them on your check sheet. Inspect porch walls and ceiling as you would those of any interior room.

GARAGES
Frequently garages are allowed to deteriorate. Inspect the walls, framing, roof, and concrete floor for major cracks, rotten wood, and leaks. Open and close doors to ensure that they lock and operate properly. Note whether the garage is equipped with lights and functioning electrical outlets. If the garage is equipped with a furnace, check to see whether it's working.

Peeling paint on windowsill caused by water

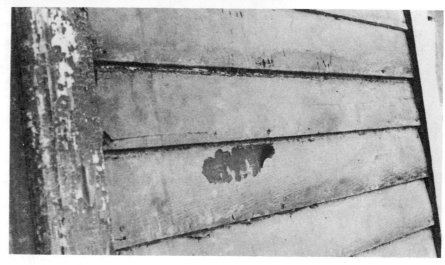

Excessive weathering on wood siding

(Source: Forest Products Laboratory, Forest Service, USDA)

89

ROOF AND EXTERIOR CHECK SHEET

ROOF: asphalt shingles _____ tile _____ wood shingles _____

rolled roofing _____ metal _____ built-up _____ other _____

condition, good _____ weathered _____ damage, location _____

_____

CHIMNEYS, CORNICES: condition, good _____ poor _____

repairs indicated, location _____

GUTTERS AND DOWNSPOUTS: serviceable _____ need cleaning _____

leaking, location _____

DRAINAGE, GROUND SLOPE: splashblocks _____ downspout extension _____

dry wells _____ low spots, location _____

WOOD IN CONTACT WITH GROUND: location _____

evidence of termites _____ decay _____ none _____

EXTERIOR WALLS: brick _____ block _____ stone _____ shingles _____

board _____ panels _____ other _____

condition, good _____ poor _____ foundations cracked _____

repairs needed, location _____

paint required, location _____

caulking required, location _____

PORCHES AND STAIRS: concrete _____ masonry _____ wood _____

condition, good _____ poor _____

GARAGE: satisfactory _____ roof leaks _____ framing, poor _____

walls cracked _____ floor, driveway cracked _____

doors, operate _____ poor _____ electrical, satisfactory _____

poor _____ none _____

OBSERVATIONS:_____

SEE BACK OF BOOK FOR DETACHABLE CHECK SHEETS

CHAPTER TEN: EVALUATING YOUR RESULTS

Congratulations! You've completed your inspection and you know more about a house and how it works than you ever did before. You're probably exhausted, too, so if you have a lot of red marks on your check sheets to consider, it's a good idea to take a break for dinner or relaxation before coming to a decision about the house.

When you return to the question, go through the check sheets and make a list of the items marked in red. Separate them into categories according to whether they are minor repairs or major defects. While everyone's opinion of minor and major will vary, among the minor ones include window latches that don't work, cracks around window frames that need to be caulked, and rough wall surfaces from an old leak, now repaired. Stopped-up drains may either be minor or be a symptom of a major problem—such as an obstructed main drain that might have to be dug up. Decide whether these are items to ask the seller to repair,

91

whether you are willing to fix them yourself, or if you will hire someone to repair them.

Larger problems, and those that the seller refuses to correct at his expense, can in turn be put into several categories: A) those you might be able to live with, provided they aren't getting any worse (for example, cracks in the foundation or walls); B) questions of insufficient services (for example, an antiquated electrical system), suspiciously aged or deteriorated items like an old furnace or a weatherbeaten roof; C) serious damage or defects so numerous as to make it uneconomical to repair them all.

You may wish to seek expert opinions. Don't ask the seller or broker to guess the cost of replacement or repairs. A factor of optimism naturally comes into their estimates. Call a contractor with the appropriate specialization. A furnace company will be able to certify your furnace as sound (if it is so) for thirty or forty dollars. An electrician, plumber, or general contractor can give you a free estimate of the cost of necessary repairs. You can obtain the services of a structural engineer to report on the foundation and walls for less than you might think. Whenever you solicit the opinion of any outside experts, advise both the broker and seller of your intention to do so under the provisions of your contract with the seller.

IF YOU WANT TO REMODEL
You may intend to undertake extensive remodeling yourself. Perhaps you've heard of people who started off on the path to riches this way. If so, the bibliography at the end of this book suggests some useful handbooks. If this is your first remodeling project, however, let me pass on a word of friendly advice: start with fairly straightforward projects that require a minimum of skills to learn and new tools to buy, like painting, wallpapering, minor sheetrock work, and laying vinyl flooring. Many people who attempt a major remodeling project as their first attempt never finish it to their satisfaction (or that of the unfortunates who buy the house after them). Most of the dogged few who do finish the job well are too exhausted, and wise enough not to start another one.

You can depend on the project taking longer than you anticipate, especially if you have only weekends and evenings and you intend a major restoration. The expense, likewise, will be greater than your original estimate. The inconvenience and worry, especially if you have to live in the house while you work on it—and who can afford to pay two mortgages?—can destroy your peace of mind or your marriage.

Restoring damaged wall surfaces, putting up and texturing sheetrock, require experience to do well. Renovating an old bathroom or a kitchen by installing new fixtures, appliances, cabinets, and countertops involves a sound knowledge of plumbing, carpentry, and decorating.

Contrary to popular belief, you may come out cheaper and better by hiring a good contractor than by trying to do it yourself. A contractor has several advantages. He can estimate the time and expense of the project more accurately than you can. He can buy materials and fixtures cheaper, at contractor's prices, and he knows just what he will need. He is less likely to waste materials. Unlike you, he won't have to buy the tools for the job, as he already has them.

If you decide to hire a contractor, ask for recommendations from friends or consult the Better Business Bureau. Don't automatically take the lowest bid for the job. The lowest bidder has to make a living too. He will probably furnish poorer quality material or hire less skilled workers, and if he runs out of money on the job, he can leave it unfinished and you will have to run the risks of suing him. He may be able to defend himself by saying that he gave you what you paid for.

Wherever possible, specify the kind and quality of materials your contractor will use, especially with roofing, kitchen cabinets, countertops, and bathroom fixtures. It's advisable to do this with paint, wallpaper, and carpet too.

Whether you remodel or not, you'll be taking care of your house from now on. Here's a list of reminders of things to do to keep your house in good condition.

RECOMMENDATIONS FOR GOOD HOUSE CARE

1. Never water next to a foundation wall.

2. Keep gutters, downspouts, and splashblocks clean and in good repair.

3. Ventilate attics and crawl spaces.

4. Use time-lag 15 amp fuses in fuse boxes, unless you positively know the circuit will handle a greater load.

5. Don't use a maze of extension cords when an additional outlet or two is called for.

6. Keep trim and exterior wood painted to protect it from weather.

7. Drain sediment from hot water heater twice a year, more frequently in hard-water regions.

8. Replace furnace filters in a warm-air system at least twice yearly.

9. Install smoke detectors and keep them in working order.

BIBLIOGRAPHY

Selected works on home construction, remodeling, repair, and related subjects for the homeowner. (United States Government pamphlets with stock numbers may be ordered directly from the Superintendent of Documents, United States Government Printing Office, Washington, D. C., 20402. A subject guide to home improvement publications will also be furnished upon request.)

GENERAL MAINTENANCE AND REPAIR

Complete Do-it-Yourself Manual (Reader's Digest, 1973). Discusses all aspects of home repair, including electrical, plumbing, heating, cooling, and exterior work.

Green, Floyd, and Susan E. Meyer, *You Can Renovate Your Own Home* (Doubleday, 1978). How to undertake major remodeling projects.

Sunset Books, *Basic Home Repairs* (Lane Publishing, 1971). A real bargain; easy-to-understand descriptions of how things work, and instructions for common, necessary repairs.

Stockwell, John, and Herbert Holtze, *How To Be a Fix-it Genius Using Seven Simple Tools* (McGraw-Hill, 1975). Novel approach, good advice on most home repair jobs — patching holes, repairing foundations, replacing glass, etc.

There are many excellent and economical government publications on these subjects. A selection follows:

Drainage Around Your Home (USDA, 1975) 001-000-03455-3.
In the Bank or Up the Chimney? A Dollars and Cents Guide to Energy-saving Home Improvements (1977) 023-00-00411-9.
Paint and Painting (GSA, 1971) 022-000-00140-0.
Painting: Inside and Out (USDA, 1978) 001-000-03874-5.
Simple Home Repairs . . . Outside (USDA program aid no. 1193).
Simple Home Repairs . . . Inside (USDA, 1973) 001-000-02815-4.
Tips for Energy Savers (Federal Energy Administration, 1977) 1977-0-244-894.
Wood Decay in Houses (USDA, 1969) 19730-497-153.

CONSTRUCTION AND REMODELING

Anderson, L. O., and O. C. Heyer, **Wood Frame House Construction** (USDA, 1955) 1960-0-304696.

Criswell, Clyde Agnew, **Masonry** (Frederick Drake, 1958).

Holtz, Wesley G., and Stephen S. Hart, **Home Construction on Shrinking and Swelling Soils** (available for 30¢ in postage from Colorado Geological Survey, Room 715, 1313 Sherman St., Denver, CO 80203).

Krieger, Morris, **Homeowner's Encyclopedia of House Construction** (McGraw-Hill, 1978). Comprehensive discussion of construction standards, heating, plumbing, electrical systems, etc. An expensive and technical, but thorough, book.

Lang, Andy, **101 Select Dream Houses** (Hammond, 1972). Custom house designs from the House of the Week series.

Lang, Andy, **Vacation Dream Homes** (Hammond, 1975). Plans for second homes; tips on financing, cost, legal aspects, construction.

Schuler, Stanley, **All Your Home Building and Remodeling Questions Answered** (Macmillan, 1971). Good on beginning construction, dealing with lenders and contractors.

Sherwood, Gerald E., **New Life for Old Dwellings** (USDA, 1975) 001-000-02988-6.

PLUMBING, HEATING, AND WIRING

Plumbing (Time-Life Books, 1976). A first-rate guide to understanding the subject; well illustrated, for the beginner.

Sessions, K. W., **The Homeowner's Handbook of Plumbing and Repair** (Wiley, 1978). Good do-it-yourself guide to repair, including useful sections on troubleshooting pumps, pressure tanks, and home water systems.

Septic Tank Care (HEW, 1973) 1973 0-521-731.

Treating Farmstead and Rural Home Water Systems (USDA, 1977) 001-000-03558-4. A valuable government publication.

Heating and Cooling (Time-Life Books, 1977). How to install and maintain heating and cooling systems, including how to add a solar water heater.

Simons, Joseph W., ***Home Heating Systems, Fuels, Controls*** (USDA, 1975) 001-000-03470-7. Good comparison and explanation of various systems.

Soderstrom, Neil, ***Heating Your Home with Wood*** (Harper & Row, 1978). For the fortunate few; how to choose fireplaces, how to clean chimneys and stovepipes.

Fireplaces and Chimneys (USDA, 1971) 001-000-01520-6.

Richter, H. P., ***Wiring Simplified*** (Park Publishing, 1971).

SOLAR INSTALLATIONS

Keyes, John H., ***Consumer Handbook of Solar Energy*** (Morgan & Morgan, 1979). Includes warnings about deceptive practices in the solar heating industry.

Sunset Magazine, ***Homeowner's Guide to Solar Heating*** (Lane Publishing, 1979).

INDEX

BASEMENT CHECK SHEET

EVIDENCE OF MOISTURE: on floor _____ walls _____ other _____ none _____

FLOOR: concrete _____ other _____ condition, good _____ fair _____
poor _____ cracked _____ badly cracked _____ heaved _____

WALLS: concrete _____ block _____ brick _____ plaster _____ other _____
cracks _____ mortar missing _____

DECAY OR INSECT DAMAGE: yes _____ not visible _____
location _____

VENTILATION: adequate _____ not adequate _____

INSULATION: under floor _____ on walls _____ on pipes _____
none _____ vapor barrier present _____

COLUMNS: steel _____ wood _____ masonry _____ other _____
not visible _____ condition, good _____ poor _____

GIRDERS: steel _____ wood _____ none _____ not visible _____
condition, good _____ poor _____

FLOOR JOISTS: size and spacing _____ condition, good _____
poor _____ not visible _____

SUBFLOOR: planks _____ plywood _____ condition, good _____ poor _____
not visible _____ leak _____

OBSERVATIONS: _____
_____